Glues, Brews, and Goos

Glues, Brews, and Goos

Recipes and Formulas for Almost Any Classroom Project
Volume 2

Diana F. Marks

Illustrated by Donna L. Farrell

2003
Teacher Ideas Press
Libraries Unlimited
A Member of Greenwood Publishing Group, Inc.
Westport, Connecticut

Dedicated to Peter, Kevin, and Colin,
my obliging sages and supports.

Teacher Ideas Press
A Division of Libraries Unlimited, Inc.
A Member of Greenwood Publishing Group, Inc.
88 Post Road West
Westport, CT 06881
www.lu.com

Production Editor: Jason Cook
Copy Editor: Ramona Gault
Layout and Interior Design: Kay Minnis

Library of Congress Cataloging-in-Publication Data

Marks, Diana F.
  Glues, brews, and goos : recipes and formulas for almost any classroom project / Diana F. Marks ; illustrated by Donna L. Farrell.
    p. cm.
  Includes bibliographical references (p. 177).
  ISBN 1-56308-362-0 (vol. 1); 1-56308-960-2 (vol. 2)
  1. Activity programs in education—Handbooks, manuals, etc.
I. Title.
LB1027.25.M26   1996/2003
372.5—dc20
                                                95-38995

Contents

Chapter 3 ■ Paints 26

Chapter 4 ■ For the Birds 39

Chapter 5 ■ For the Bugs 43

Chapter 12 ■ Activities About Other Times and Other Cultures 74

Chapter 13 ■ Face and Body Paints 83

Chapter 14 ■ Recycled Paper and Paper Projects 87

Chapter 15 ■ Growing Plants 96

Chapter 16 ■ Science Projects 103

Chapter 17 ■ Snow Globes 115

Chapter 18 ■ Geology Fun 118

Chapter 19 ■ Making Musical Instruments 122

Chapter 24 ■ Pickles, Sauerkraut, Mustards, and Horseradish 161

Chapter 25 ■ Treats That Students Can Make . . . 168

Chapter 26 ■ Miscellaneous 185

Acknowledgments

I want to thank my husband, Peter, for his support and encouragement. He knows when to help and when to leave me alone.

I thank my sons, Kevin and Colin, and all their friends for helping me try out so many ideas.

I thank my students at Wrightstown Elementary School. I appreciate their enthusiasm and their concern for their "resident author."

Introduction

I lied. In 1996 I published a book, *Glues, Brews, and Goos: Recipes and Formulas for Almost Any Classroom Project*. Notice the words *almost any,* like what else is left to write about? Since 1996 I kept finding more great projects and recipes and formulas. I kept wishing I had included this or that. So in the summer of 2001 I contacted my publisher to see if I could write a sequel, if you will. So began *Glues, Brews, and Goos: Recipes and Formulas for Almost Any Classroom Project, Part 2.*

This book stands alone; you do not need the first volume to use it. All these ideas have been kid-tested and teacher-approved (that's me). Although some of this book's recipes and activities are centuries old, there are no repeats from the first book.

The purpose for creating this book is the same as for the first book: To provide activities that help students become interested, avid learners. Learning should reflect real life and be stimulating. Students like to feel and taste and smell. They like to be involved. After learning about different kinds of rocks, they can make volcanic rock candy and then eat it. They can mummify an apple and grow sweet potato plants. They can taste cinnamon crisps and smell homemade horseradish. They can make clouds disappear and make crystals appear.

This book will help students realize how lucky they are to live in the twenty-first century. They can pick up a ballpoint pen and write a letter. This book will show them how to make the quill pen, paper, ink, and letter seal that students used in 1776. Today's students can buy all kinds of fancy party decorations, or they can follow the instructions about making paper garlands and flower balls. They can pour factory-made syrup on previously frozen pancakes, or they can make pancakes from scratch and top them with homemade syrups.

Another of my goals is to help students feel a part of the global society. They will see that Navajo fry bread is not so different from a French crepe or an Indian chappati. They can taste matzo ball soup for Passover and hamantaschen for Purim. They can try crumpets and sopapilla and pemmican.

I hope that students will experience the "ooh" and "aah" of science. Here they will find the ways to make needles into compasses, potatoes into paper, and berries into ink. They can see that the art of making pickles relies on the science of making a brine. They will find out that the presence of large amounts of sugar in strawberry jam actually keeps away bad microbes. They will help various kinds of birds and learn how to attract moths. They will find out that music depends on the science of sound and that art media are reflections of the science of light and optics.

Since students always love to eat, I have included quite a few food recipes. They can make Irish potato candy for St. Patrick's Day, mints for Valentine's Day, and marshmallow ghosts for Halloween. Maybe on some cold winter morning they can make hot cocoa and doughnuts for the whole class. They can make gifts of peanut butter turtles for Mother's Day and containers of honey mustard for Father's Day.

I want students to understand the world around them and that they can change that world. They can find out how a thermometer works and how a camera takes pictures. They can see how helicopters fly. They can measure the speed of wind and find its direction as well. These students will hopefully be experimenters and risk takers when they grow up. The Nobel Prizes are waiting for them.

Finally, students need the opportunity to be creative and playful. Therefore, I have included many recipes for just that. Students can make their own stickers and paint on windows. They can form art objects from sawdust and play a kazoo. They can whip up inks that disappear and buttons that hum and flowers that last for years.

I had fun writing this book. I hope you have fun using it. I hope that this book is used so much it becomes stained and dog-eared. Good luck on your journey through life and learning.

Tips

- Always test a formula before using it with students.

- Check to make sure all materials are gathered together before beginning a project.

- Make safety the top priority. Try to anticipate any possible problems and eliminate all dangers. Review safety procedures with students.

- Keep pots, spoons, and utensils used for making food separate from those used in non-food projects.

- Recipes and formulas note when a stove or heating element is required. However, electric frying pans and pots, if available, are preferable. Temperatures can be controlled more accurately on electric appliances, and they can be used right in the classroom.

- Because hot running water is not available in many classrooms, cleaning up can be difficult. If running water is not available, use plastic bags to hold ingredients instead of mixing bowls. Students like to seal the bags and mix the contents by squeezing. Though plastic bags are not the most environmentally preferred material, their use may make the difference between carrying out a project or dismissing it as too cumbersome.

- Keep notes on what works and what does not work with your students.

- Experiment and enjoy!

1
Clays and Doughs

Clays and doughs can be divided into two groups, those that dry and those that do not dry. A clay or dough that dries will retain its shape and be used to make permanent projects. A dough that does not dry can keep its shape if left undisturbed. However, it can be used only for temporary activities. Most of the recipes included here will dry. Each recipe indicates whether the clay will dry or not.

The following clays and doughs do not require a kiln. Clays and doughs can clog a sink, so they should be thrown away in the trashcan.

■ Real Clay
[Makes about 5 cups]

Real clay is often found along riverbanks or washed-out areas. Squeeze together what you think might be clay. If it sticks together when you release your hand, it probably is clay. While real clay products can be placed in a kiln, they can also be just left to dry.

Materials

about 6 cups clay
bucket
3 layers newspaper
hammer
old sieve

old bowl
cloth big enough to line the bowl
water
flat surface
container with a tight lid

Procedure

1. Fill the bucket with the clay.
2. Pour the clay onto the layers of newspaper and let it dry thoroughly.
3. Remove any debris such as rocks or twigs.
4. Use the hammer to break up the clay.
5. Sift the dry clay through the old sieve to remove small pieces of debris.
6. Pour the clay back into the bucket and cover with water. Let the mixture sit for about a day.
7. Discard any extra water. Pour the clay into the old bowl lined with cloth.
8. Allow the clay to dry enough so that it is easy to work with.
9. Now wedge the clay to get out any air bubbles. To wedge the clay, pick it up and throw it on the work surface until no more air bubbles are present.
10. Store the clay in a container with a tight lid.

■ Very Easy Flour Dough
[Makes about 3½ cups]

As a clay, this material does not keep for any length of time. The finished pieces do dry.

Materials

3 cups flour
3 tablespoons powdered tempera
    paint
½ cup cooking oil

water
mixing bowl
mixing spoon
wax paper

Procedure

1. Combine the flour, powdered tempera paint, and cooking oil in the mixing bowl.
2. Add enough water to make a soft dough.
3. Create objects and let them air dry on wax paper.

■ Flour and Sugar Dough
[Makes about 2½ cups]

As a clay, this material does not keep for any length of time. The finished pieces do dry.

Materials

1 cup flour
1 cup sugar
1 cup water
1 cup boiling water

old pot
heating element
mixing spoon
wax paper

Procedure

1. Combine the flour, sugar, and 1 cup water in the old pot.
2. Pour in boiling water and cook for 5 minutes, stirring continuously.
3. Cool.
4. Create objects and let air dry on wax paper.

■ Bread Dough

[Makes about ½ cup]

Only small objects can be made with this recipe. This clay does dry. Save the bread crusts for treats for the squirrels.

Materials

2 slices day-old bread
2 tablespoons white glue
3 drops glycerin

4 drops white vinegar
bowl
food coloring

Procedure

1. Tear off the bread crusts and crumble bread into small pieces in the bowl.

2. Add the white glue, glycerin, and white vinegar.

3. Mix together until the dough is supple and smooth.

4. Add food coloring and blend it into the dough.

5. Make small objects and dry. Drying can take 2 days.

■ Dryer Lint Clay

[Makes 4 cups]

Students can collect dryer lint for a couple of weeks before the project. Commercial laundries may be able to give you lots of lint. The oil of wintergreen keeps the clay from becoming moldy. Finished pieces will dry.

Materials

3 cups dryer lint
2 cups water
⅔ cup flour
3 drops oil of wintergreen
    (for preservative)*

newspaper
pot
heating element
mixing spoon

*Oil of wintergreen should not be eaten. If young students use this material, consider leaving the oil out.

Procedure

1. Combine lint and water in the pot.

2. Stir in the flour and the oil of wintergreen.

3. Stir over low heat until the mixture is stiff.

4. Take it out of the pot and place it onto the newspaper to cool.

5. Fashion into objects. The objects will dry within a day or two.

■ Clay Beads
[Makes about 2 cups]

This clay is easy to work with. Interesting patterns can be created. The beads do dry.

Materials

2 cups baking soda
1 cup cornstarch
1¼ cups water
pot
heating element
mixing spoon

small containers
food coloring
plastic wrap
drinking straws
wax paper

Procedure

1. Combine the cornstarch and baking soda in the pot.
2. Stir in the water.
3. Heat the mixture at medium, stirring constantly until it forms a dough. This takes about 10 to 15 minutes.
4. Take the pot off the heating element and allow the clay to cool.
5. Divide into sections and place each portion in a separate container. Add a few drops of food coloring to each portion.
6. Cover each container with plastic wrap until you are ready to use it.
7. Break off pieces and roll into beads.
8. Use the drinking straws to make holes through the beads.
9. Place the beads on the wax paper to dry. It may take overnight to make them very hard.

■ Sand Beads

[Makes 1 cup]

Students like the grainy texture. It is messy at first, but it is worth the time. The beads do dry.

Materials

1 cup sand	several smaller containers
¼ cup white glue	tempera paints
disposable container	toothpicks
disposable mixing spoon	wax paper

Procedure

1. Combine the sand and white glue in the disposable container.
2. Divide mixture between several small containers and add tempera paints if desired.
3. Pinch off bits of clay to make beads.
4. Use the toothpicks to make the holes for the beads.
5. Dry at least overnight on wax paper.

■ Flower Petal Clay Beads

[Makes about 1½ cups]

Six cups of flower petals is quite a bit. Students could collect flower petals during late summer. Floral shops may provide discarded blossoms. The beads do dry.

Materials

6 cups flower petals	old mixing bowl
⅔ cup flour	mixing spoon
2 tablespoons salt	toothpicks
⅓ cup water	wax paper

Procedure

1. Crumble and tear the petals into small pieces. They will soften and smell wonderful.
2. Combine the flour, salt, and water in the mixing bowl.
3. Work in the flower petals until the dough is soft and fun to work with.
4. Tear off small pieces of dough and roll into balls.
5. Use the toothpicks to make holes through the beads.
6. Place the beads on the wax paper. Let them air dry for a day or two.

■ Sawdust Clay 1
[Makes 2½ cups]

Lumberyards will donate lots of sawdust. The trip to collect the sawdust is interesting. No smoking is allowed near the sawdust because tiny particles fill the air and are easily combustible. The sawdust creations do dry.

Materials

2 cups sawdust
1 cup wallpaper paste
¼ cup plaster of paris*

water to moisten
old dishpan
wax paper

*Plaster of paris may be hazardous to health if used extensively without protection. Students should perhaps use plaster of paris outside. If used inside, students should perhaps wear goggles and dust filter masks.

Procedure

1. Combine the sawdust, wallpaper paste, and plaster of paris in the old dishpan.
2. Add enough water to make a stiff dough.
3. Create objects and let air dry on wax paper.

■ Sawdust Clay 2
[Makes 1 cup]

Finished products can be sanded.

Materials

1 cup sawdust
1 cup thin paste or paper paste
food coloring (optional)

newspaper
old mixing bowl
old cookie sheet

Procedure

1. The sawdust can be dyed by adding some food coloring. Spread the sawdust on the newspaper to dry.
2. Combine the sawdust and paste in the old mixing bowl.
3. Use like a clay and fashion into objects.
4. Let air dry for 2 or 3 days, or bake on an old cookie sheet at 200° F for 1 to 2 hours.

■ Sawdust Clay 3

[Makes about 2½ cups]

Sift through the sawdust to take out large pieces. This clay does produce hard, finished items.

Materials

2 cups sawdust
1 cup flour
water

old dishpan
wax paper

Procedure

1. Combine the sawdust and flour in the old dishpan.
2. Add enough water to make a stiff dough.
3. Fashion mixture into objects and place on wax paper.
4. Dry materials in the sun.

■ Glue-Dextrine Dough

[Makes enough dough for 3 small pieces]

Dextrine is found in artificial sweeteners. These can be purchased at a grocery store. Finished items will dry.

Materials

1 teaspoon Sobo or other white
    household glue
1 cup powdered dextrine
1 tablespoon hot water
¼ cup plaster of paris*, patching
    plaster, whiting, Bon Ami,
    unscented talcum, or powdered
    chalk

palette knife or putty knife
old plate
small bowl
disposable spoon
wax paper

*Plaster of paris may be hazardous to health if used extensively without protection. Students should perhaps use plaster of paris outside. If used inside, students should perhaps wear goggles and dust filter masks.

Procedure

1. Pour Sobo glue or other white household glue on the plate.
2. Combine the dextrine and hot water in the small bowl.
3. Add dextrine solution to the glue and mix well.
4. Add plaster of paris 1 tablespoon at a time. Mix with the palette knife and keep adding plaster until no more can be absorbed.
5. Knead the dough and shape into desired objects.
6. Allow objects to dry on wax paper.

■ Sweet-Smelling Dough

[Makes 3 cups, enough for 2 or 3 projects]

This dough has a bright, sparkly color and a pleasant smell. Consider adding glitter or bits of plastic confetti. Items produced from this dough will dry.

Materials

2¼ cups flour
1 cup salt
2 tablespoons unsweetened powdered
    drink mix
4 tablespoons oil

1 cup water
large mixing bowl
mixing spoon
kneading surface with extra flour
airtight storage container

Procedure

1. Combine the flour, salt, and unsweetened powdered drink mix in the large mixing bowl.
2. Add oil and water.
3. Stir until mixture is stiff.
4. Place dough on floured kneading surface and knead for two minutes or until it is smooth and pliable.
5. Store in an airtight container.
6. Creations will air dry after a couple of days.

■ Cotton Ball Dough

[Makes about 3 cups]

Cotton ball dough makes great snowmen and winter dioramas. Items will dry.

Materials

3 cups cotton balls
2 cups water
1 cup flour
food coloring

old pot
heating element
mixing spoon
paper towels

Procedure

1. Shred cotton balls into small pieces.
2. Pour cotton ball pieces into pot and add water.
3. Add the flour little by little, stirring all the time.
4. Cook over low heat for about 5 minutes until mixture becomes stiff.
5. Remove the dough from the pot and place on paper towels to cool.
6. Mold when cool.
7. Shapes will harden within a day.

■ Coffee Clay
[Makes about 2½ cups]

Coffee clay has a nice smell and an interesting texture. Baked items will become hard.

Materials

¼ cup instant coffee
¾ cup warm water
2 cups flour

½ cup salt
mixing bowl
mixing spoon

Procedure

1. Dissolve the coffee in a small portion of the warm water.

2. Add the flour and salt to the mixture.

3. Add the rest of the warm water and stir until the dough is pliable.

4. Bake products at 300° F for 30 minutes or until hard.

■ Construction Paper Modeling Compound
[Makes about 3 cups]

This mixture can go sour if left too long before using.

Materials

2 cups colored construction paper,
    torn into small bits
4 cups water
½ cup flour

blender
mixing bowl
mixing spoon
kneading surface with extra flour

Procedure

1. Combine the construction paper bits and 3½ cups water in the blender. Blend about 30 seconds until a pulp forms.

2. Remove the excess water.

3. Combine ½ cup water and the flour in the mixing bowl.

4. Gradually add paper pulp to flour/water mixture.

5. Knead until it forms a stiff clay.

6. Finished products will dry within a day or two.

■ Whole Wheat Flour Dough 1
[Makes 4 to 4½ cups]

This dough produces a light brown, speckled product. It is very appealing to students.

Materials

2¼ cups boiling water
2 cups salt
3 cups flour
1 cup whole wheat flour

mixing bowl
kneading surface with extra flour
old cookie sheet

Procedure

1. Combine the boiling water and salt in the mixing bowl. Stir until the salt is dissolved.
2. Slowly add the flours, stirring after every addition. Make a stiff dough.
3. Knead on a floured surface. Fashion into objects.
4. Bake objects at 275° F for about 2 hours.
5. Objects can also air dry over several days.

■ Whole Wheat Flour Dough 2
[Makes 4 cups, enough for 4 students]

Students should keep their hands wet when they mix this clay. The moisture keeps the dough from sticking to their hands.

Materials

1 cup salt
1½ cup water
2 tablespoons oil
5 cups whole wheat flour

mixing bowl
mixing spoon
cookie sheet

Procedure

1. Combine the water and salt in the bowl.
2. Stir in the oil and flour.
3. Form desired shapes.
4. Place on baking sheet and bake at 325° F for 1 hour.

■ Coffee Grounds Rocks

[Makes about 2½ cups, enough for about 10 rocks]

Collect the coffee grounds from the faculty room coffeepot at the end of the day. Leave them out to dry overnight.

Materials

1 cup coffee grounds	mixing bowl
1 cup flour	mixing spoon
½ cup sand	wax paper
½ cup salt	cookie sheet
1 cup water	

Procedure

1. Combine the coffee grounds, flour, sand, and salt in the mixing bowl.
2. Add enough water to make a stiff dough.
3. Scoop out pieces of dough the size of golf balls and shape as desired. Place on wax paper. They will air dry within 3 days.
4. Or bake on cookie sheet at 150° F for about 25 minutes.

■ Crepe Paper Molding Material

[Makes about 1 cup]

Colored crepe paper pulp may stain hands and clothing. Consider adding several drops of vanilla extract or other flavoring to mask the rather unpleasant smell.

Materials

1 roll of crepe paper	⅓ cup salt
water	mixing bowl
old bucket	mixing spoon
½ cup flour	

Procedure

1. Shred the crepe paper into small bits and place the bits in the old bucket.
2. Cover the crepe paper with water and let the mixture soak overnight.
3. Thoroughly remove the water and transfer one cup of pulp to the mixing bowl.
4. Add the flour and salt and stir until the ingredients are thoroughly mixed.
5. Mold as if it were papier-mâché.

■ Permanent Sand Clay

[Makes about 2½ cups]

Students like this clay's texture. Could this be done outdoors?

Materials

2 cups sand
⅔ cup cornstarch
1½ cups liquid starch
old pot

heating element
mixing spoon
kneading surface covered with wax paper.

Procedure

1. Pour the sand and cornstarch into the old pot.

2. Mix in the liquid starch.

3. Stirring constantly, cook over medium heat until a dough forms.

4. Remove from heat and let cool.

5. Knead mixture for about one minute before molding.

■ Zonalite Carving Compound

[Makes about 3 cups]

This grainy carving compound is a new experience for many students. This compound produces hard finished items.

Materials

1 cup Zonalite*
1 cup sand
2 cups plaster
water

old bucket
half-gallon wax-carton milk container,
    empty and clean
carving tools

*Zonalite is similar to vermiculite and can be bought at hardware stores and plant nurseries.

Procedure

1. Combine the Zonalite, sand, and plaster in the old bucket.

2. Slowly add water to the bucket, mixing as you add. Stop adding water when the mixture is the consistency of pudding.

3. Pour into container and let harden at least 2 days.

4. Peel away the container and carve.

■ Ice Sculptures

[Makes enough for 10 sculptures]

This makes a great project for cold winter mornings and hot summer afternoons.

Materials

10 disposable aluminum pie pans   water
10 cups of clay   food coloring (optional)

Procedure

1. Line pie pan with clay to form a creative mold.
2. Fill the mold with water and add food coloring if desired.
3. Place in a freezer.
4. The next day take the pans from the freezer and remove the clay.
5. Place the sculptures outside if it is cold enough.

■ Chocolate Clay

[Makes about ¾ cup]

What can we say? Students can have their clay and eat it, too!

Materials

10 ounces chocolate chips or discs   mixing spoon
⅓ cup corn syrup   wax paper
microwave-safe bowl   tray
microwave oven

Procedure

1. Pour the chocolate into the microwave-safe bowl and microwave until the chocolate is melted (about 2 to 3 minutes).
2. Add corn syrup and mix.
3. Place wax paper on tray.
4. Pour mixture on wax paper and spread. Cover loosely with wax paper and allow to stiffen (about 2 hours).
5. Play and eat.

■ Frozen Bread Molding Material

[Makes enough for 4 students]

This dough can be expensive. Watch for sales. Baking produces hard-finished items that will not be eaten.

Materials

1 loaf of frozen bread dough
1 egg white
2 teaspoons water
cookie sheet
enough cooking oil or shortening to
    coat cookie sheet

small mixing bowl
fork
brush

Procedure

1. Defrost bread dough the day before using.
2. Break dough into smaller portions and shape as desired.
3. Place creations on greased cookie sheet.
4. Let rise for about 1 hour.
5. Beat egg white and water together in mixing bowl with the fork.
6. Brush the egg white on creations.
7. Bake at 350° F for about 15 to 20 minutes.

■ Cinnamon Dough

[Makes about 1½ cups]

The smell is wonderful! It does not easily dry out. Consider making Christmas items from the material.

Materials

1 cup flour
½ cup salt
2 teaspoons cream of tartar
2 teaspoons cooking oil
1 cup water
about 6 drops red food coloring
about 6 drops green food coloring
2 tablespoons cinnamon

2 tablespoons allspice
2 mixing bowls
2 mixing spoons
old pot
heating element
kneading surface with extra flour
small container with lid

Procedure

1. Mix the flour, salt, and cream of tartar in one bowl.

2. Stir in the cinnamon and allspice.

3. In the other bowl, add the food colorings to the water. Red and green should form brown.

4. Add the colored water and the oil to the dry ingredients and stir.

5. Pour into old pot and cook the mixture for about 3 minutes, stirring constantly.

6. Remove the dough from the pot and knead until it is pliable and smooth.

7. Allow to cool.

8. Store in a small container. Make sure the lid is tight.

9. Shape as desired.

■ Spicy Fried Dough
[Makes about 2½ cups]

This project requires lots of effort, but it is worthwhile. Obviously, these creations do not last long.

Materials

1 teaspoon cinnamon
½ teaspoon nutmeg
2 cups flour
2 teaspoons baking powder
⅓ cup sugar
⅓ cup milk

3 tablespoons cooking oil
mixing bowl
mixing spoon
wax paper
frying oil
deep fryer

Procedure

1. Combine the cinnamon, nutmeg, flour, baking powder, and sugar in the mixing bowl.
2. Add the milk and 3 tablespoons cooking oil.
3. Knead until dough forms a ball.
4. Divide into portions and place on pieces of wax paper.
5. Mold into desired shapes.
6. Fry in oil at 375° F until brown.
7. Eat!

■ Pickle Juice Dough
[Makes about 6 cups]

The smell is wonderful! The idea is unusual! This dough does not dry.

Materials

2½ cups pickle juice or vinegar
¾ cup baking powder
5 cups flour
5 tablespoons cooking oil

tempera paint
mixing bowl
mixing spoon
smaller containers

Procedure

1. Combine the pickle juice, baking powder, flour, and cooking oil in the mixing bowl.
2. Divide among several containers.
3. Add paints until desired shades are reached.
4. Mold as desired.

2
Glues and Pastes

What is the difference between a glue and a paste? I think a glue can be poured or squeezed on. I think a paste has to be applied with a brush or other tool. Both glues and pastes demonstrate adhesion and cohesion. The glue has to stick to itself (cohesion), and it has to stick to the surfaces it is gluing (adhesion).

■ Homemade Glue
[Makes about 1 cup]

This glue is very useful, but it must rest for at least 12 hours before it can be used.

Materials

2 tablespoons corn syrup	old pot
2 teaspoons white vinegar	heating element
¾ cup water	2 mixing spoons
½ cup cornstarch	mixing bowl
¾ cup very cold water	airtight container

Procedure

1. Combine corn syrup, vinegar, and ¾ cup water in pot and heat until it begins to boil.
2. Combine the cornstarch and ¾ cup very cold water in the mixing bowl.
3. Slowly add the cornstarch-water mixture to the mixture in the pot.
4. Stir until thoroughly mixed.
5. Remove from heat and let it rest overnight.
6. Store in an airtight container.

■ Homemade Paste
[Makes 1 pint]

Homemade paste will last for 2 or 3 months without being refrigerated; it is a good paste to use with papier-mâché.

Materials

¼ cup sugar
½ cup flour
½ teaspoon alum
1¾ cup water
¼ teaspoon oil of cinnamon (for preservative)*

old pot
heating element
mixing spoon
brush
storage container

*Oil of cinnamon should not be eaten. If young students make this paste, consider leaving the oil out.

Procedure

1. Combine the sugar, flour, and alum in the old pot.
2. Stir in 1 cup water.
3. Boil, stirring until the mixture is clear.
4. Stir in ¾ cup water and the oil of cinnamon.
5. Pour into storage container and let cool.
6. Apply with brush.

■ Sticker Gum 1

[Makes ¼ cup]

Students have fun with this recipe. They can make their own stickers.

Materials

1 tablespoon (1 packet) unflavored
    gelatin
1 tablespoon sugar
¼ cup boiling water
½ teaspoon flavoring (such as vanilla
    or strawberry)

small mixing bowl
spoon
old paintbrush
small storage container with lid

Procedure

1. Combine gelatin and boiling water in small mixing bowl.
2. Add sugar and flavoring.
3. Let cool for a few minutes and then pour into small storage container.
4. Store in refrigerator or it will mold.
5. To use, place container in warm water to liquefy gum. Paint surface with a bit of the mixture.
6. Let dry. Moisten to activate the stickiness.

■ Sticker Gum 2

[Makes ¼ cup]

This recipe has a strong, pleasant smell.

Materials

¼ cup hot water
3 tablespoons flavored gelatin
mixing bowl

spoon
old paintbrush
small cutouts from magazines

Procedure

1. Pour the gelatin into the bowl.
2. Add the hot water and stir until thoroughly mixed.
3. Paint solution on backs of cutouts and allow to dry for about an hour.
4. Moisten back of cutout to activate.

■ Molding Paste

[Makes about 4 cups]

This paste sort of turns paper into papier-mâché.

Materials

1 cup flour
5 tablespoons sugar
4 cups water
old pot

heating element
mixing spoon
container with lid

Procedure

1. Combine the ingredients in the old pot.
2. Stir until the mixture boils.
3. Reduce the heat. Keep stirring until the mixture becomes thick.
4. Remove from the heat and pour into the container. Let paste cool.
5. Refrigerate any unused portion in closed container.

■ Quick Molding Paste

[Makes about 1½ cups]

This recipe requires no heat, and it is extremely easy to make.

Materials

1 cup flour
1 cup water
mixing bowl

mixing spoon
container with lid

Procedure

1. Combine the flour and water in the mixing bowl until the mixture is thick.
2. Store unused portion in closed container in the refrigerator.

■ Sugar Glue

[Makes about 2 cups]

This glue is a good emergency glue when a project is due right away and the commercial glue is all gone.

Materials

½ cup sugar
½ cup flour
1½ cups water
old pot

heating element
mixing spoon
container with lid

Procedure

1. Combine the flour, sugar, and water in the old pot.

2. Stirring constantly, bring the mixture to a boil.

3. Reduce the heat and cook until the mixture is thick.

4. Pour into container and allow to cool. Cover with lid.

5. Store unused portion in the refrigerator.

■ Cornstarch Squeeze Glue

[Makes 2 cups]

The cornstarch-water mixture can act either as a liquid or as a solid. Thus it becomes a good glue.

Materials

3 tablespoons cornstarch
4 tablespoons water
2 cups hot water
old pot

heating element
mixing spoon
clean squeeze bottle such as an old dish detergent bottle

Procedure

1. Combine the cornstarch and 4 tablespoons water in the old pot.

2. Stir in the 2 cups hot water.

3. Heat at a medium temperature until the mixture thickens.

4. Remove from the heat and let cool.

5. Pour into the squeeze bottle.

6. Refrigerate when it is not being used.

■ Casein Glue
[Makes about ¾ cup]

The ancient Egyptians made casein glue thousands of years ago.

Materials

1 quart skim milk
1 cup vinegar
old pot
heating element
wooden spoon
strainer
cheesecloth

old construction paper
airtight container
disposable cup
1½ tablespoons hot water
2 teaspoons borax
brush

Procedure

1. Combine the skim milk and vinegar in the old pot.
2. Heat the mixture over low heat for about 15 minutes until a film forms on top.
3. Place the cheesecloth in the strainer and pour the liquid from the pot into the strainer.
4. Run water through the strainer to remove any remaining vinegar.
5. Remove the cheesecloth and curd from the strainer and squeeze out any remaining liquid.
6. Remove the curd and place between sheets of old construction paper for at least a day.
7. Remove the curd and place it in the airtight container.
8. To make casein glue, dissolve 2 teaspoons borax into 1½ tablespoons of hot water in a disposable cup.
9. Add 2 tablespoons of the curd. Combine and let cool for a minute or two. Apply the glue with a brush.

■ Envelope Glue
[Makes about ½ cup]

Students can make their own envelopes from a sheet of paper and this glue.

Materials

6 tablespoons white vinegar
4 tablespoons (4 packets) unflavored
    gelatin
1 teaspoon vanilla extract
old pot

heating element
mixing spoon
airtight container
old brush

Procedure

1. Pour vinegar into the pot and bring to a boil.
2. Dissolve gelatin in vinegar.
3. Add extract to provide flavor.
4. Pour into airtight container.
5. When ready to use, transfer a small amount of the glue into a paper cup. Place the paper cup in a larger cup containing hot water. The heat will melt the solid glue into a liquid. Brush the liquid glue onto the envelope flap.

■ Transparent Mending Glue
[Makes 1½ pints]

This glue repairs torn pages in books. To use, place a small amount of the glue over the tear and apply a small piece of white tissue paper. The tissue paper will become transparent when the glue dries.

Materials

¾ cup rice flour
2 tablespoons sugar
¾ cup water
2½ cups hot water
½ teaspoon oil of wintergreen
    (as preservative)*

old pot
heating element
mixing spoon
airtight container

*Oil of wintergreen should not be eaten. If young students make this glue, consider leaving the oil out.

Procedure

1. Combine the rice flour, sugar, and ¾ cup water in the old pot.
2. Add the 2½ cups hot water.
3. Bring mixture to a boil, stirring constantly until it is the consistency of pudding.
4. Allow to cool and add oil of wintergreen.
5. Pour into the airtight container and refrigerate.

3
Paints

Paint is made by combining a pigment (color) with a binder (viscous material). The binder makes the pigment adhere to the support (paper, wood, or other materials). Four types of paints are nontoxic and are thus safe for students to use. Food coloring (not actually a paint) is transparent. However, it will not always wash out of clothes, and it can temporarily stain fingers. Watercolors are transparent and usually washable. Tempera and poster paints are more opaque. They are reasonably priced and easy to obtain. They often wash out of clothing. Acrylics are expensive, and they can sometimes ruin clothing. In most cases, you can interchange the paints to meet your needs.

Finger paint paper can be bought from most craft catalogs. Freezer paper and shelf paper are easier to obtain and usually work just as well. Different types of watercolor paper are available. But keep in mind that most of these paints are designed to work on ordinary white drawing paper.

■ Easiest Finger Paint
[Makes enough for 4 containers of ¼ cup each]

The name gives it away. It dries with a nice sheen. Laundry starch can be found in the detergents aisle of the grocery store.

Materials

1 cup liquid laundry starch	small containers with lids
food coloring or powdered tempera paints	mixing spoon

Procedure

1. Pour ¼ cup liquid laundry starch into each of 4 containers.
2. Add food coloring or powdered tempera paint until desired shade is reached.

■ Easy Finger Paint

[Makes about 2¼ cups]

Colored sand can be added instead of food coloring or tempera paints.

Materials

2 cups water
½ cup flour
food coloring or tempera paints
microwave-safe container

microwave oven
spoon
small containers with lids

Procedure

1. Combine the flour with a small amount of water in the microwave-safe container until it makes a paste.
2. Add the rest of the water, stirring continually.
3. Microwave the mixture for 3 minutes. Stir and microwave again for 3 minutes.
4. Pour the mixture into the small containers. Add food coloring or tempera paints and mix until desired shades are produced.
5. Refrigerate.

■ Smelly Finger Paint

[Makes 2 tablespoons of finger paint]

These paints obviously have nice smells. They feel good on fingers, and the final product has a shiny, grainy finish. You may substitute 1 tablespoon (1 envelope) unflavored gelatin, several drops of food coloring, and several drops of flavoring in place of the flavored, sugar-free gelatin.

Materials

1 small package flavored sugar-free gelatin
2 tablespoons hot water

small mixing bowl
mixing spoon

Procedure

1. Combine the gelatin and hot water in the mixing bowl.
2. Let cool for about 15 minutes.
3. Use paints in one setting; these paints cannot be stored.
4. Paintings will usually dry overnight.

■ Classic Finger Paint
[Makes about 2½ cups]

This recipe is very old. It is worth the effort.

Materials

1 cup flour
3 tablespoons salt
1½ cups water
1¼ cups hot water
food coloring

old pot
heating element
mixing spoon
small containers with lids

Procedure

1. Combine the salt, flour, and 1½ cups water in the old pot.
2. Stirring constantly, heat the mixture.
3. Slowly add the 1¼ cups hot water.
4. Stirring constantly, bring the mixture to a boil. Remove from heat when it is thick.
5. Pour the mixture into the containers. Add food coloring until the desired shade is reached.
6. Store in the refrigerator.

■ Soap Flake Finger Paint
[Makes about 1 cup]

This paint does well on dark paper.

Materials

¼ cup soap flakes
½ cup warm water
food coloring

egg beater
bowl
small containers with lids

Procedure

1. Pour the warm water into the bowl.
2. Slowly add a small amount of the soap flakes to the water. Beat.
3. Repeat the process until all the soap flakes have been added and the concoction looks like whipped cream.
4. Divide the mixture into several small containers and add food coloring until desired shade is reached.

■ Window Finger Paint

[Makes 1¼ cups]

This finger paint is nice and thick. It produces an opaque picture on windows, and it is very easy to wash off.

Materials

1 cup baby shampoo
½ cup cornstarch
mixing bowl

mixing spoon
small containers
food coloring

Procedure

1. Combine the baby shampoo and cornstarch in the mixing bowl.

2. Divide the mixture into several small containers and add food coloring until desired shade is reached.

■ Cornstarch Finger Paint

[Makes about 2½ cups]

The glycerin gives it a nice flow.

Materials

½ cup cornstarch
¾ cup water
2 cups hot water
2 teaspoons boric acid
(for preservative)*
1 tablespoon glycerin

food coloring or tempera paints
old pot
heating element
mixing spoon
small containers with lids

*Boric acid should not be eaten. If young students make this paint, consider leaving the boric acid out.

Procedure

1. Combine ¼ cup water with cornstarch in the old pot to make a paste.

2. Stir in 2 cups hot water.

3. Heat at a low temperature, stirring constantly until mixture starts to boil.

4. Add ½ cup water, boric acid, and glycerin.

5. Pour into small containers and add food coloring or tempera paints until desired colors are reached.

■ Laundry Starch Finger Paint
[Makes 2 cups]

Laundry starch can be found in the detergents aisle of the grocery store.

Materials

¼ cup water
¼ cup laundry starch
1½ cups hot water
2 tablespoons talcum powder
¼ cup soap powder
½ teaspoon boric acid
    (for preservative)*

food coloring or tempera paints
old pot
heating element
spoon
small containers with lids

*Boric acid should not be eaten. If young students make this paint, consider leaving the boric acid out.

Procedure

1. Combine the laundry starch and cold water in the old pot.

2. Pour in the hot water and stir.

3. Over low heat, cook until the mixture is thick. Stir constantly.

4. Remove from the heating element and add talcum powder, soap powder, and boric acid.

5. Pour into small containers and add food coloring or tempera paints until desired colors are reached.

■ Edible Finger Paint
[Makes 4 cups]

This paint actually dries if it is applied lightly to the paper. Youngsters of all ages enjoy using this paint. Consider adding a flavoring to the plain yogurt.

Materials

1 container plain yogurt
food colorings
small dishes

spoons
wax paper

Procedure

1. Spoon some of the plain yogurt into the small dishes.

2. To each dish add food coloring until desired shades are reached.

3. Students can paint on the wax paper and lick their fingers as they go.

■ Sidewalk Paint

[Makes enough for 4 containers of ¼ cup each]

The next rain will wash away this paint.

Materials

1 cup cornstarch
1 cup water
food coloring or powdered tempera
    paints

small containers with lids
mixing spoon

Procedure

1. Combine ¼ cup water with ¼ cup cornstarch in each of 4 containers.

2. Add food coloring or powdered tempera paints until desired shade is reached.

■ Spritz Paint

[Makes 1 cup]

This paint can be spritzed on snow or sand. The next rain will wash it off.

Materials

1 cup water
5 tablespoons cornstarch
food coloring
1 spritz bottle (can use an empty,
    clean window cleaner bottle)

small mixing bowl
spoon

Procedure

1. Combine the cornstarch and water in the small mixing bowl.

2. Add food coloring and mix until desired shade is reached.

3. Pour into spritz bottle.

■ Gouache
[Makes ¾ cup]

A gouache is a heavy, opaque watercolor. This recipe requires dextrine, which is found in artificial sweeteners. These can be purchased at a grocery store.

Materials

2 cups dextrine   powdered tempera paints
4 tablespoons water   jar
½ cup honey   spoon
2 teaspoons glycerin
½ teaspoon boric acid
    (as preservative)*

*Boric acid should not be eaten. If young students make this paint, consider leaving the boric acid out.

Procedure

1. Combine the dextrine and water in the jar.
2. Stir in honey, glycerin, and boric acid. Thoroughly combine all ingredients.
3. Add powdered tempera paints until the desired color is reached.

■ Puffy Paint
[Makes about 1 cup]

This paint makes a great accent to projects. Colored sand and glitter can be used as substitutes for plain sand.

Materials

½ cup salt   mixing bowl
½ cup flour   spoon
½ cup water   paper or plastic cups
powdered tempera paints   plastic squeeze bottles
1 tablespoon sand

Procedure

1. Combine salt and flour in mixing bowl.
2. Add water and sand.
3. Divide mixture among four or more cups.
4. Add powdered tempera paints until desired shades are reached.
5. Pour each paint into a plastic squeeze bottle.
6. Squeeze paints onto paper or hard surfaces.
7. Let dry at least overnight and perhaps longer.
8. Refrigerate leftover paints, but bring back to room temperature before using.

■ Mucilage Paint
[Makes 1 cup]

Mucilage is a type of glue. This paint sticks nicely to cardboard.

Materials

½ cup mucilage	jar with lid
½ cup honey	powdered tempera paints

Procedure

1. Combine the mucilage and honey in the jar. Shake until well mixed.
2. Add powdered tempera paints until the desired color is reached.

■ Thick Milk Paint
[Makes ½ cup]

The colonists used milk as their binder because it was available and cheap.

Materials

½ cup condensed milk	spoon
food coloring	small containers with lids
small mixing bowl	

Procedure

1. Combine the condensed milk and food coloring in small mixing bowl.
2. Store in small airtight containers.

■ Casein Paint
[Makes ¾ cup]

The milk provides the casein. This recipe was used by people centuries ago.

Materials

½ cup warm water	powdered tempera paints
2 tablespoons borax	jar with lid
¼ cup powdered nonfat milk	spoon

Procedure

1. Combine the borax and water in the jar.
2. Add the powdered milk and stir. Mixture should be thick.
3. Add powdered tempera paints until the desired color is reached.

■ Scratch-and-Sniff Paint

[Makes 1 tablespoon]

Students could make their own valentines and add a scratch-and-sniff accent.

Materials

2 tablespoons unsweetened powdered drink mix

1 tablespoon warm water

small paper cup

mixing spoon

Procedure

1. Combine drink mix and water in cup.

2. Paint on surface.

3. Allow surface to dry for 24 hours before scratching and sniffing.

■ Shaving Cream Paint and Sculpting Material

[Makes enough for 10 students]

The finished sculptures are delicate and temporary. This project is fun, and students enjoy the smell.

Materials

1 can white shaving cream

food coloring

small paper cups

plastic spoon

Procedure

1. Squirt some shaving cream into each of the paper cups.

2. Carefully mix in several drops of food coloring.

3. Create sculptures and let dry.

■ Dish Soap Paint

[Makes 2½ tablespoons of one color]

This paint can last a long time. It is incredibly easy to make and fun to use.

Materials

2 tablespoons clear dish soap
2 tablespoons powdered tempera
    paint
1 teaspoon water

small mixing bowl
spoon
small containers with lids

Procedure

1. Mix the soap, powdered tempera paint, and water in the small bowl.

2. Store in small containers. Make sure lids are on tight.

■ Syrup Paint

[Makes 3 tablespoons of one color]

This paint actually dries, and it is very glossy. Colors are very vibrant. It can be used as a finger paint.

Materials

3 tablespoons light corn syrup
food coloring
small mixing bowl

spoon
small containers with lids

Procedure

1. Combine the light corn syrup and at least 6 drops of food coloring in small mixing bowl.

2. Store in small containers. Make sure lids are on tight.

■ Pan Paint

[Makes ⅓ cup base to be divided into several portions, one for each color]

The mixture will foam at first. This recipe lets the students design their own colors.

Materials

3 tablespoons cornstarch
3 tablespoons baking soda
3 tablespoons white vinegar
2 teaspoons light corn syrup

food coloring
mixing bowl
mixing spoon
several containers with lids

Procedure

1. Combine the cornstarch, baking soda, white vinegar, and light corn syrup in the mixing bowl.

2. Place a small amount of the mixture into each of several containers.

3. Add food coloring to achieve desired shade.

4. Use as is or wait until they dry into pan paints. To use pan paint, moisten a paintbrush and apply it to the paint. The brush will pick up the paint.

■ Laundry Starch Paint

[Makes about 1½ cups]

Laundry starch can be found in the detergents aisle of the grocery store.

Materials

1 cup laundry starch
1 cup soap powder
3 tablespoons powdered tempera
   paint

1 cup water
mixing bowl
mixing spoon
airtight container

Procedure

1. Combine the laundry starch, soap powder, and powdered tempera paint in the mixing bowl.

2. Add the water and mix until smooth.

3. Store in airtight container.

■ Detergent Paint

[Makes about ¾ cup]

This paint has a grainy texture until the detergent fully dissolves.

Materials

1 cup powdered detergent
6 tablespoons liquid tempera paint
¼ cup water

mixing bowl
mixing spoon
airtight container

Procedure

1. Combine the powdered detergent and liquid tempera paint in the mixing bowl.

2. Add ¼ cup water a tablespoon at a time. Stir. The mixture should be the consistency of pudding.

3. Pour into airtight container.

4
For the Birds

■ Springtime Nest-Building Material

Place the materials outside a classroom window so that students can see the birds in action. Students may want to save their dryer lint over winter to have enough for the spring.

Materials

scraps of yarn or string about 5 inches long

lint from clothes dryer

Procedure

1. Loosely tie the scraps of string or yarn to branches of trees.
2. Place the dryer lint where birds can reach it.
3. The birds will use this material to build their nests.

■ Popsicles for Birds

[Makes 1]

Birds need water even in the winter. They can get some moisture from the melting water.

Materials

birdseed
cranberries
large paper cup

scrap of string or yarn
water

Procedure

1. Pour some birdseed and cranberries into the cup.
2. Fill with water.
3. Place the 2 ends of the string into the water to form a handle.
4. Place in the freezer for about a day.
5. When frozen, take out and hang on a branch.
6. Watch the birds come for their frozen treats.

■ Treats for Birds

[Makes 1]

Save the bread scraps and give them to the squirrels.

Materials

slice of bread

peanut butter

birdseed

large cookie cutter

drinking straw

string

Procedure

1. Apply the cookie cutter to the slice of bread and remove the shape.
2. Spread peanut butter on the shape.
3. Sprinkle with birdseed.
4. Poke a hole at the top with the drinking straw.
5. Let the shape dry overnight.
6. Put a piece of string through the hole and tie to a branch.
7. Stand back and watch the birds enjoy their treat.

■ Bird Energy Cakes

[Makes 5]

Birds need fat, especially in winter. This mixture gives them the fat to keep up their energy.

Materials

2 cups melted shortening

1 cup peanut butter

2 cups corn meal

old mixing bowl

old mixing spoon

5 empty, clean yogurt containers

knife

string

Procedure

1. Combine the melted shortening and peanut butter in the old mixing bowl.
2. Add the corn meal slowly and thoroughly combine with the fat and peanut butter.
3. Use the knife to punch 2 small holes near the top of each yogurt container.
4. Thread string through the holes and tie knots in the strings.
5. Spoon some of the mixture into each of the yogurt containers.
6. Allow the mixture to cool.
7. Tie the filled containers to tree branches or bird feeders.

■ S'mores for Birds
[Makes 6]

Most birds love graham crackers.

Materials

6 graham crackers   ½ cup raisins
½ cup peanut butter   knife

Procedure

1. Spread the peanut butter on the graham crackers.
2. Sprinkle raisins on top of the peanut butter.
3. Place the s'mores in bird feeders.

■ Fruit Kabobs for Birds
[Makes 6]

Each fruit kabob also provides a perch for the birds so that they can rest and eat.

Materials

about 2 pounds of fruit pieces (such   knife
   as apples, peaches, pears, or   6 very small disposable pie plates
   plums)
6 pieces of string, each about 30
   inches long

Procedure

1. Use the knife to punch a small hole through the center of the bottom of each pie plate.
2. Thread the string through the bottom of the pie plate and make a knot below the pie plate so the string won't slip through the hole.
3. Use the knife to make small holes in the pieces of fruit.
4. Thread the string through the fruit. The fruit should rest in the pie plate when you are done.
5. After the fruit has all been strung, tie the kabobs to tree branches.

5
For the Bugs

■ Butterfly Cage (temporary home)
[Makes 1]

This is really an activity for two people. It is difficult to keep embroidery hoops in the right places. Netting can be purchased at a fabric store. It comes in quite a few lovely colors.

Materials

1 yard netting
2 embroidery hoops

4 pieces of yarn, each 12 inches long
1 piece of yarn about 2 feet long

Procedure

1. Spread the netting out on a flat surface.
2. Place 1 embroidery hoop in the middle of the netting.
3. Gather the netting around the hoop.
4. Hold the other hoop about 6 inches above the first hoop.
5. Tie the second hoop to the netting with the 4 pieces of yarn.
6. Draw up the netting so that a bag is formed.
7. Tie the ends of the netting together with the long piece of yarn. Then suspend the cage from a wire.

■ Critter Cage (temporary home)
[Makes 1]

Netting could be substituted for the panty hose.

Materials

1 quart milk carton, empty and clean
old panty hose

rubber band
scissors

Procedure

1. Cut two openings in opposite sides of the milk carton.
2. Add whatever materials your critter might need (water, leaves, etc.).
3. Cut off a leg of the panty hose and put the milk carton inside the leg.
4. Add your critter.
5. Pull the panty hose leg completely over the milk carton and fasten shut with the rubber band.
6. Trim off any excess panty hose.

■ Moth Attractor Goo
[Makes 1 batch]

Moths are mostly night insects. The attractor goo can be prepared during the day, but a night visit is essential to see the moths.

Materials

2 cups orange juice that has been at room temperature for about 2 days
4 overripe bananas
½ cup honey or corn syrup

mixing bowl
mixing spoon
plastic wrap
old paintbrush
flashlight

Procedure

1. Place the peeled bananas in the bowl and mash with the back of the mixing spoon.
2. Add the orange juice and combine.
3. Add the honey or corn syrup and combine.
4. Cover the bowl with plastic wrap and allow it to sit outside in the sun for several hours.
5. Take the mixture and the old paintbrush to where several trees are next to open space.
6. Paint several tree trunks with the mixture.
7. After dark, return to the area and see if the moths like the mixture.

■ Butterfly Nectar
[Makes 1 quart, enough for 1 feeder for about 3 weeks]

Butterflies seek out nectar from flowers. This homemade nectar satisfies their taste buds as well. Butterflies are attracted to bright colors, especially orange and purple. Therefore, make the butterfly feeder (nectar container) bright orange and purple. Clean the container often so that the nectar does not spoil.

Materials

1 quart water
1 cup sugar
pot
heating element
mixing spoon

small, empty, clean cottage cheese
    container
sponge cut to the size of the cottage
    cheese container
airtight container with lid

Procedure

1. Pour the water into the pot and heat until it boils.
2. Turn down the heat and add the sugar. Stir and cook until all the sugar is dissolved.
3. Remove the pot from the heat and allow the solution to cool.
4. Place the sponge in the empty cottage cheese container.
5. Pour in enough nectar to saturate the sponge.
6. Place the container on a rock or ledge in a sunny part of the garden. Wait for your guests!
7. Refrigerate the remaining nectar in the airtight container with lid.
8. Replace the nectar every 3 to 4 days.

■ Food for All Kinds of Bugs
[Makes 1 cup, enough for about 3 days]

This food attracts bees and wasps as well as butterflies and ants.

Materials

1 cup overripe fruit, cut into pieces
1 small, disposable pie pan

Procedure

1. Place the overripe fruit in the disposable pie pan.
2. Put the pie pan on a rock or large piece of wood. Give your guests time to find it.

6
Crystals

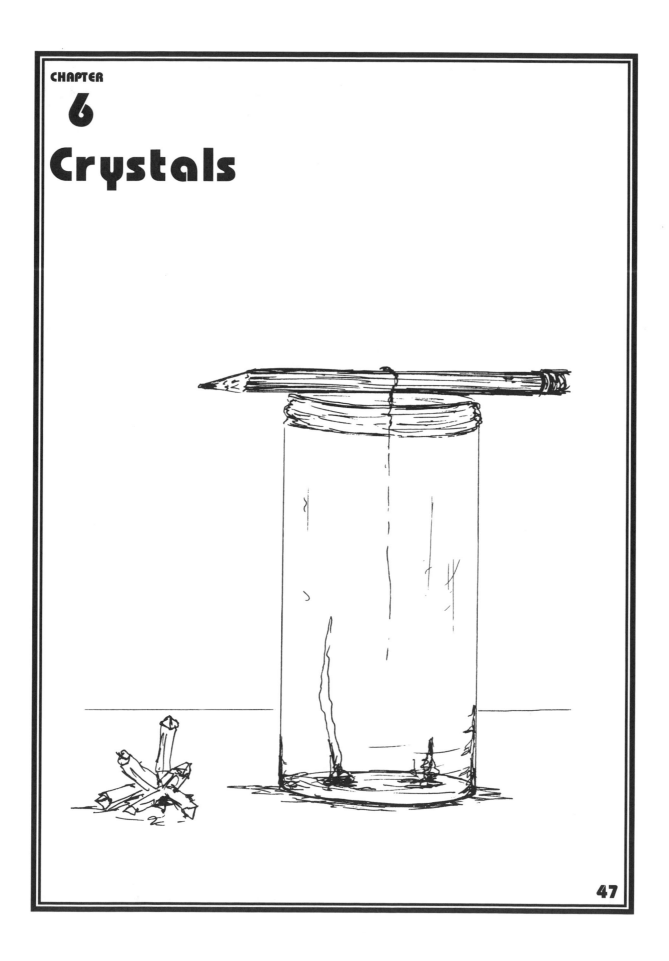

Crystals are easy to produce, and students like to see the daily changes. However, crystal solutions should not be disturbed after they are made. The two main ingredients for crystal growing are the chemical (crystal material) and water. A saturated solution is made by dissolving as much of the chemical as possible in boiling water. When the solution cools, it becomes supersaturated. Crystals are a by-product of this supersaturation.

■ Suspended Sugar Crystals
[Makes 1 experiment]

These crystals develop within a closed system. Evaporation is not part of the process.

Materials

1 envelope unflavored gelatin	pot
1 cup water	heating element
2½ cups sugar	mixing spoon
glass jar with lid	towel

Procedure

1. Combine the unflavored gelatin and water in the pot. Heat until boiling and then turn off heat.
2. Slowly stir in sugar, ¼ cup at a time, until no more sugar will dissolve.
3. Pour the liquid into the glass jar. Leave any undissolved sugar at the bottom of the pot.
4. Screw on the lid.
5. Wrap in the towel (so that the mixture will cool slowly) and place in a spot where it will not be disturbed for weeks.

■ Salol Crystals
[Makes small amount of crystal]

Salol (phenyl salicylate) can be purchased from science supply houses. The size of the crystals depends on the rapidity of the cooling process. The slower the cooling, the larger the crystals will be.

Materials

½ oz. salol (phenyl salicylate)	shallow pan of warm water
1 small glass container	small, shallow aluminum pan

Procedure

1. Place the salol in the glass jar. Warm the salol by placing the jar in the shallow pan of warm water. Make sure no water enters the jar.
2. After the salol melts, pour it into the small, shallow aluminum pan.
3. Crystals should form as the salol cools.

■ Sodium Thiosulfate Crystals

[Makes 1 batch]

Sodium thiosulfate is also known as photographer's hypo, used to develop photographs. This experiment may not always work; even a bit of dust can cause the crystals not to form.

Materials

1 box (16 ounces) sodium thiosulfate
1 glass or enamel pan
heating element
¼ cup water
mixing spoon

1 heat-proof jar, pint-sized
old towel
hot pads
piece of cardboard slightly bigger than the
     mouth of the jar

Procedure

1. Heat the water in the glass or enamel pan.
2. Save a bit of the sodium thiosulfate. Slowly add the rest of the sodium thiosulfate to the pan, stirring constantly.
3. When all the sodium thiosulfate is dissolved, carefully pour the solution into the jar.
4. Wrap the towel around the jar to slow down the cooling process.
5. Cover the mouth of the jar with the piece of cardboard. This keeps out the dust.
6. Let the solution cool to room temperature. This may take several hours.
7. Drop one speck of the sodium thiosulfate you saved into the solution. The single speck will cause the supersaturated solution to crystallize in just a few minutes.

■ Disappearing Crystals

[Makes 1 experiment]

Soil Moist crystals are polymers, which are long chains of atoms formed by joining identical groups of atoms. This particular polymer soaks up water to become 300 to 400 times its original size.

Materials

about 15 Soil Moist crystals
    (available at nurseries)
2 glass jars, 1 with lid

distilled water
aluminum pie pan
string

Procedure

1. Place about 15 Soil Moist crystals in one jar and fill with distilled water to about ½ inch from the top.

2. Screw on the lid and wait a few hours. The crystals should have really grown.

3. Place several on the aluminum pie plate. Choose one and gently tie a string around it.

4. Fill the other jar with distilled water and lower the crystal into it. Wait a few hours again. The crystal should disappear until someone pulls on the string and removes the crystal.

■ Homemade Geodes

[Makes 12]

Students enjoy making these shiny gems. If kept dry, the crystals can last quite a long time.

Materials

1 empty, clean egg carton
plastic wrap
scissors
clean, empty eggshell halves,
    obtained by cracking open eggs
    and draining the contents

supersaturated solution of salt or Epsom
    salts

Procedure

1. Cut the plastic wrap into 12 pieces and line each of the 12 depressions in the egg carton.

2. Place an eggshell half in each depression.

3. Pour some supersaturated solution into each of the eggshell halves.

4. Let mixture sit for several days. The eggshell halves should start to look like geodes.

■ Bath Crystals
[Makes 1 batch]

These would make nice Mother's Day presents. Washing soda (sodium carbonate) can be found in the laundry products section of the grocery store.

Materials

1 cup washing soda crystals
plastic storage bag
food coloring
fragrance

small amount of water
eyedropper
wax paper
glass or plastic jar with lid

Procedure

1. Pour the washing soda crystals in the plastic bag.
2. Add a few drops of water and two drops of food coloring to the washing soda crystals.
3. Close the bag and shake so that the color becomes uniform throughout the crystals.
4. Open the bag. Add the fragrance, close the bag, and shake again.
5. Pour the crystals onto the wax paper and allow to dry for about 10 minutes.
6. Pour the crystals into the jar and seal.
7. To use, place a small amount of the crystals into bath water.

7

Non-Newtonian Fluids and Slimes

Non-Newtonian fluids fascinate students. These fluids have properties of both solids and liquids. They resemble liquids because they take the shape of their containers. They resemble solids because they can maintain a definite shape. In the 1700s Isaac Newton developed a description of Newtonian fluids (fluids that "behave," meaning they take the shape of their container and they flow when the container is tilted) and non-Newtonian fluids, substances that do not "behave." Ketchup and quicksand are non-Newtonian fluids. Non-Newtonian fluids can clog drains, so never use a sink to dispose of such materials.

■ Gelatin Goo
[Makes 1 cup]

Food coloring and/or flavorings could be added to this mixture.

Materials

½ cup boiling water
3 tablespoons (3 packets) unflavored
   gelatin
½ cup light corn syrup

mixing bowl
mixing spoon
fork

Procedure

1. Pour the boiling water into the mixing bowl.
2. Add the gelatin and let it soften for several minutes.
3. Mix in the gelatin.
4. Add the light corn syrup and mix.
5. Use the fork to pull out strands of goo.
6. This does not preserve well, so play with it the day it is made.
7. Do not pour this mixture down any drain.

■ Stretchers

[Makes 4 tablespoons]

Students really enjoy playing with these.

Materials

2 tablespoons white glue	2 small mixing bowls
food coloring	spoons
1 tablespoon (1 packet) unflavored	cookie cutter
gelatin	wax paper
2 tablespoons boiling water	

Procedure

1. Combine food coloring and white glue in one bowl.
2. Dissolve gelatin in the boiling water in another bowl.
3. Combine the two mixtures and stir until the batch thickens.
4. Pour mixture into cookie cutter that is placed on wax paper.
5. Allow to stand until the mixture is firm.
6. Remove from mold and dry 1 hour on each side.
7. Students can now investigate their stretchers.
8. If allowed to dry, the stretchers become hard.

■ Fake Plastic

[Makes about 1 cup]

This wonderful material is opaque.

Materials

¼ cup water	kneading surface with extra flour
food coloring	2 small mixing bowls
¼ cup white glue	mixing spoons
½ cup cornstarch	wax paper
½ cup flour	

Procedure

1. Combine the liquids in one mixing bowl.
2. Combine the flour and cornstarch in the other bowl.
3. Add the flour/cornstarch mixture to the other mixture and stir until the dough becomes stiff.
4. Turn the mixture out onto the kneading surface (with extra flour on it) and knead for several minutes.
5. Mold creations and place on wax paper.

■ Epsom Salts Goo
[Makes enough for 1 student]

This goo is fun to make for a Halloween haunted house. Students are sometimes reluctant to touch the goo.

Materials

3 tablespoons white glue
1½ teaspoons Epsom salts
1½ teaspoons water

1 disposable cup
1 disposable spoon
paper towels

Procedure

1. Combine the Epsom salts and water in the disposable cup.
2. Add the white glue.
3. Stir the mixture.
4. Pour it out on the paper towel to absorb the extra moisture.
5. Knead the mixture until it becomes gooey.

■ Squeeze Goo
[Makes about 1½ cups]

This goo makes nice accent touches to projects. It is fun to make and use.

Materials

1 cup flour
¼ cup salt
¼ cup sugar
¾ cup water

food coloring
mixing bowl
mixing spoon
squeeze bottle

Procedure

1. Combine the flour, salt, and sugar in the mixing bowl.
2. Add the water.
3. Add drops of food coloring until the desired shade is reached.
4. Pour mixture into the squeeze bottle.
5. Squeeze the goo to form designs and patterns on paper. It will take a day or two to dry.

■ Gelatin Strings
[Makes about 20]

The gelatin is a colloid, somewhat like a liquid and somewhat like a solid.

Materials

1 package flavored gelatin
water
shallow pan

plastic drinking straws
knife

Procedure

1. Prepare the gelatin according to the directions on the box.
2. Pour the mixture into the shallow pan and place in refrigerator for about 30 minutes. The gelatin should be thick by then.
3. Sink the straws in the gelatin so they are lying on the bottom of the pan, and place the pan back in the refrigerator. Leave it there for a day.
4. The next day use the knife to cut the straws out of the gelatin.
5. Pinch 1 end and begin to roll up the straw so that the gelatin strings pop out of the straws. Eat!

■ Guar Gum Slime
[Makes 8 batches of about ½ cup each]

Guar gum can be bought at health food stores. It is a vegetable gum that is used to thicken foods and cosmetics.

Materials

2 teaspoons guar gum
1 tablespoon borax
1 cup water
1 quart warm water
2 mixing bowls

2 mixing spoons
2 empty, clean plastic milk jugs with lids:
     1 one-quart and 1 half-gallon
8 disposable cups
8 disposable spoons

Procedure

1. Combine the borax and 1 cup water in the mixing bowl. Pour into the one-quart milk jug.
2. Pour 1 quart warm water into the second mixing bowl. Add about 1 teaspoon of the guar gum and stir until dissolved.
3. Continue to add small amounts of the guar gum to the warm water until all the guar gum is dissolved.
4. Pour the guar gum and water mixture into the half-gallon milk jug.
5. To make the slime, pour ½ cup of the guar gum solution into a disposable cup.
6. Add 1 teaspoon of the borax mixture, and stir.
7. The slime will last for a day or two. Then it reverts back to mostly liquid.

8

Bubbles and Bubble Solutions

Most bubble solutions should be made days ahead, preferably even a week ahead, of when you plan to use them. Keep bubble solutions at room temperature. Use distilled water whenever possible. The size of the bubbles depends on such factors as humidity and air circulation. Also, the rule seems to be that less is more where bubbles are concerned. The less soap used, the bigger the bubbles. If bubbles are used indoors, watch out for slippery floors by the end of the project.

■ Oil Bubbles
[Makes 1 cup]

The cooking oil extends the life of the bubbles.

Materials

⅔ cup water, preferably distilled
⅓ cup liquid dishwashing detergent
1 teaspoon cooking oil

mixing bowl
mixing spoon
container with lid

Procedure

1. Combine the water, dish detergent, and cooking oil in the mixing bowl.

2. Pour into container and allow it to age for at least 24 hours.

■ Liquid Starch Bubbles
[Makes ½ cup, enough for 1 student]

The mixture may at first be a bit thin, but it will thicken. Laundry starch can be found in the laundry products section of the grocery store.

Materials

½ cup liquid laundry starch
about 1 tablespoon liquid
    dishwashing detergent

paper cups
bubble wands

Procedure

1. Pour the liquid starch into a paper cup.

2. Add a generous dash of dish detergent to the liquid starch.

3. Dip in the bubble wands and watch the results.

■ Liquid-Filled Bubbles

[Makes 1 batch]

The liquid-filled bubbles actually have a layer of air surrounding them. This layer keeps the liquid inside from spreading into the surrounding liquid.

Materials

½ cup corn syrup	1 glass bowl
water	spoon
1 teaspoon dishwashing detergent	1 measuring cup
4 drops food coloring	1 clean, empty squeeze bottle
½ teaspoon salt	

Procedure

1. Pour the corn syrup onto the bottom of the glass bowl. This layer will hopefully protect the liquid-filled bubbles as they fall.
2. Gently pour water into the bowl.
3. Add the dish detergent and gently swirl the mixture to distribute the detergent.
4. Use the measuring cup to scoop out some of the water-detergent mixture.
5. Add the food coloring to the water-detergent mixture in the measuring cup. The color will help you see the liquid-filled bubbles.
6. Add the salt to the measuring cup and stir until dissolved. The salt will help the bubbles sink.
7. Pour the salt-food coloring-water-detergent mixture into the squeeze bottle and screw on the top.
8. Hold the opening of the squeeze bottle vertical to the bowl and gently squeeze.
9. Some of the liquid-filled bubbles will fall below the surface of the water in the bowl.
10. It is fun to watch the bubbles sink and then rise to the surface.

9
Invisible Inks

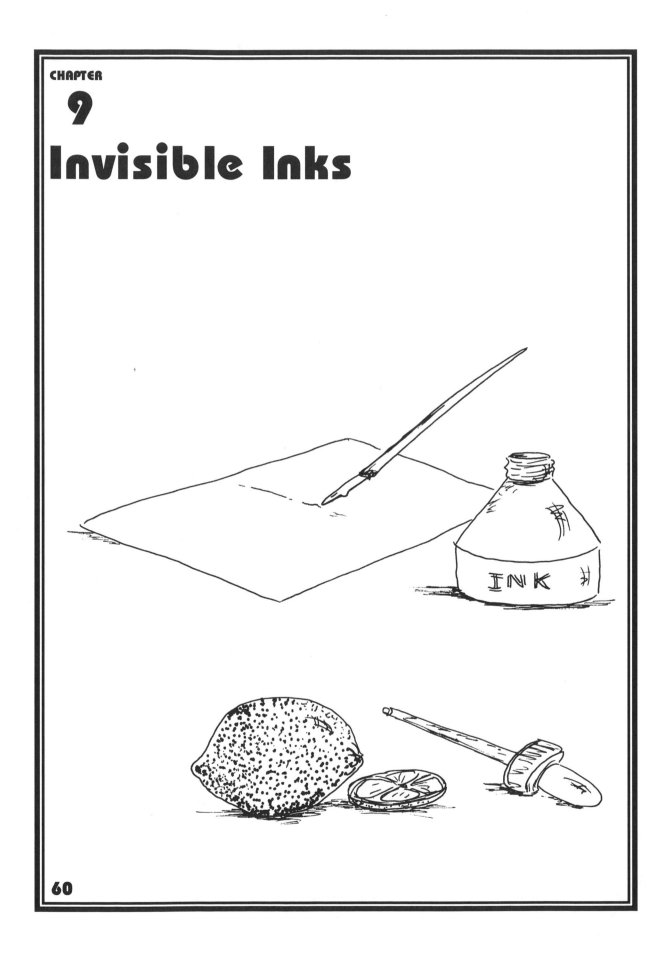

Invisible inks have been around for hundreds of years. Most are chemical reactions. For example, iodine reacts with starch, and a base reacts with an acid.

■ Wax Invisible Ink
[Makes 1]

Emergency candles can be purchased at hardware stores. Old candles with not much color could be substituted. This project is an example of a "resist." The wax resists the water in the watercolors.

Materials

1 clear emergency candle	1 set watercolors and brush
1 piece construction paper	water

Procedure

1. "Write" a message on the construction paper with the candle. The more wax used, the more successful the product will be.

2. To reveal the message, apply watercolor paints on top of the paper. The wax should resist the watercolors, and the message will appear.

■ Cornstarch Invisible Ink
[Makes ¼ cup]

This process works because the iodine reacts with the starch in the cornstarch.

Materials

1 teaspoon cornstarch	10 drops iodine*
½ cup water	disposable container
microwave-safe bowl	paper
microwave oven	2 swabs
mixing spoon	

*Iodine is poisonous and flammable. Supervise its use carefully. It can be purchased at pharmacies.

Procedure

1. Combine the cornstarch and ¼ cup water in the microwave-safe bowl.

2. Microwave for about 30 seconds to thicken mixture.

3. Write a message on the paper with the cornstarch mixture, using a swab. Let the paper dry.

4. Combine the iodine and ¼ cup water in the disposable container.

5. With the second swab, paint the paper with the iodine mixture. The message will appear in dark blue or purple.

■ Baking Soda Invisible Ink

[Makes about ¼ cup]

The grape juice concentrate contains acids. These acids react with the baking soda, which is a base.

Materials

¼ cup baking soda
¼ cup water
small bowl
mixing spoon

¼ cup grape juice concentrate
2 swabs
paper

Procedure

1. Combine the baking soda and water in the small bowl.

2. Use one swab to write a message with the mixture on the paper. Wait for the paper to dry.

3. Use the second swab to paint the paper with the grape juice concentrate. The message should appear.

■ Vinegar–Red Cabbage Invisible Ink

[Makes ¼ cup vinegar solution and 1 cup indicator solution]

The red cabbage water acts as an indicator and reacts to acidic vinegar.

Materials

¼ cup vinegar
½ red cabbage
1 cup water
knife
pot

heating element
mixing spoon
paper
2 swabs

Procedure

1. Use a swab dipped in vinegar to write a message on the paper. Let the paper dry.

2. Cut the cabbage into small pieces and place in the pot.

3. Add the water and cook over low heat until the water turns deep red or purple. Keep the liquid.

4. Use the other swab dipped in the red cabbage liquid to cover the paper. The message should stand out.

■ Phenolphthalein Invisible Ink
[Makes ¼ cup phenolphthalein solution and ¼ cup washing soda solution]

The phenolphthalein acts as an indicator and reacts to the base in the washing soda. Washing soda (sodium carbonate) is located in the laundry products section of the grocery store.

Materials

3 laxative tablets containing phenolphthalein
½ cup water
3 tablespoons washing soda

2 small containers
mixing spoons
2 swabs
paper

Procedure

1. Place the laxative tablets in one of the small containers. Crush the tablets with the back of a spoon.
2. Add ¼ cup water and mix.
3. Combine the washing soda and ¼ cup water in the other small container.
4. Dip one swab in the liquid from the phenolphthalein and write a message on the paper. Let the paper dry.
5. Dip the other swab in the washing soda mixture and cover the paper. The message should become light pink.

■ Table Salt Invisible Ink
[Makes ¼ cup solution]

The salt and the graphite from the pencil do not seem to get along.

Materials

3 tablespoons table salt
¼ cup water
small container
mixing spoon

1 swab
1 pencil
paper

Procedure

1. Combine the table salt and water in the container. Stir until the salt dissolves.
2. Dip the swab in the saltwater solution and write a message on the paper. Let the paper dry.
3. Rub over the area with the pencil. The message should appear.

10
Candles

Many families in colonial America made candles from tallow, which is fat from cows or sheep. Today, however, most candles are made from beeswax or paraffin. Beeswax candles last longer and give a brighter light than paraffin candles, and they have a lovely fragrance. As might be expected, beeswax costs more than paraffin. To improve paraffin candles, add some beeswax to the mixture. Just 20 percent beeswax in the mixture makes a difference in the end product. If using paraffin alone, add 3 tablespoons stearic acid (which comes in a powder form) to each pound of paraffin. The stearic acid reduces smoking and makes the candle harder. Both beeswax and paraffin are available from candle-making supply houses. Paraffin can also be purchased from grocery stores and chemical supply houses.

Two types of wicks, wire and braid, are available in various thicknesses. Use thinner wicks for short or thin candles and thicker wicks for tall or wide candles. Craft stores sell many supplies to use in candle making. Items include wick holder tabs, concentrated colors, scents, mold sealers, and mold releases.

It is relatively easy to estimate how much wax is needed. Decide how much the final candles should weigh. That is the amount of wax to melt.

■ Salt Candles
[Makes 1]

The baby food jar can become hot when the candle is lit.

Materials

clean, empty baby food jar	empty can in which to melt wax
¾ cup salt	double boiler
3 colors of food coloring	water for double boiler
3 small empty yogurt containers	heating element
mixing spoons	hot pads
beeswax	candle wick about 3 inches long

Procedure

1. Distribute the salt among the yogurt containers and color with food coloring.
2. Pour each layer of salt carefully into the baby food jar. Do not mix the layers.
3. Place the beeswax in the empty can and place it in the double boiler. Add water to the double boiler. Melt the wax over low heat.
4. Use the hot pads to pour the melted wax almost to the top of the jar.
5. Let the wax cool for a few minutes and then push the wick into the jar. Allow about an inch of wick to remain above the top of the jar.
6. Allow the candle to cool completely.

■ Seashell Candles
[Each shell makes 1 candle]

These candles make good reminders of summer vacations. They are also a way to recycle nature's gifts.

Materials

several layers of newspaper	double boiler
several clean seashells	water for double boiler
mixing spoons	heating element
beeswax	hot pads
empty can in which to melt wax	birthday candles

Procedure

1. Spread the several layers of newspaper out on the working surface.
2. Place the seashells on the newspaper. Prop up any shells that might tip over with wads of newspaper.
3. Place the beeswax in the empty can and place it in the double boiler. Add water to the double boiler. Melt the wax over low heat.
4. Use hot pads to pour the wax into the seashells.
5. Let the wax cool for about five minutes.
6. Push a birthday candle into the wax as far as you can. This will form the wick of the candle. Do not worry if the top of the birthday candle shows. It will melt the first time the candle is lit.
7. Let the candles cool.

■ Squash Candles
[Makes 1]

These candles are great for harvest activities.

Materials

1 squash or gourd	water for double boiler
knife	heating element
several layers of newspaper	hot pads
beeswax	wick
empty can in which to melt wax	small washer
double boiler	

Procedure

1. Cut off the top of the squash or gourd. Remove as much flesh as possible.

2. Place the squash or gourd on the newspaper. Prop up the sides with wads of newspaper.

3. Place the beeswax in the empty can and place it in the double boiler. Add water to the double boiler. Melt the wax over low heat.

4. Tie the wick to the small washer. The washer will weigh down the wick in the hot liquid wax.

5. Lower the washer to the bottom of the squash. Make sure the free end of the wick rests on the edge of the squash.

6. Use hot pads to pour the wax into the squash.

7. Let the wax cool. Every few minutes, for an hour or so, make sure the wick is vertical.

■ Rolled Beeswax Candles

[Makes about 4]

These candles are easy to make, and they can be quite colorful.

Materials

beeswax

old crayons (with paper removed) or
    colored candle stubs

empty can in which to melt wax

double boiler

water for double boiler

heating element

small cookie sheet with lip

wax paper

hot pads

wick

small washers

old knife

Procedure

1. Place the beeswax in the empty can and place it in the double boiler. Add water to the double boiler. Melt the wax over low heat.
2. If desired, add old crayons or candle stubs for color.
3. Tie a wick to the small washers. The washers will weigh down the wick.
4. Line the cookie sheet with wax paper.
5. Use the hot pads to pour the melted beeswax onto the cookie sheet. Consider pouring 2 colors of wax next to each other and marbleizing the material with a tongue depressor.
6. Let wax cool but not harden.
7. While the wax is still warm and pliable, cut it into sections. Place the wick with washer along one edge of a section of wax.
8. Roll the wax over the wick so that ultimately the wick is in the center of the candle.
9. Stand the candle up and let it cool.

11
Dried Flowers

Flowers can be dried in many ways. Whatever the method, water must be removed. The flowers should not be placed in sunlight because it will fade the flowers' colors. Dried flowers will usually last for about a year.

■ Dried Flowers 1

[Makes 3 cups drying mixture]

This mixture can be used over and over. Borax can be bought in the detergents section of the grocery store.

Materials

1 cup borax	spoon
2 cups cornmeal	shoebox with lid
mixing bowl	fresh flowers

Procedure

1. Combine the borax and cornmeal in the bowl.
2. Spread about half an inch of the mixture in the bottom of the shoebox.
3. Gently place the flowers on top of the mixture.
4. Cover the flowers completely with more of the mixture.
5. Place the lid on the box and store at room temperature for about a month.
6. Indicate the date that you put the flowers in and the probable date they will be ready.

■ Dried Flowers 2

[Makes 3 cups drying mixture]

Borax can be bought in the detergents section of the grocery store.

Materials

3 cups borax
plastic bag
plastic bag tie

coffee can with lid
fresh flowers
soft paint brush

Procedure

1. Place the plastic bag in the coffee can.
2. Add enough borax so that about one inch of it covers the bottom of the bag.
3. Put one flower in "face down." Cover with more borax.
4. Add more flowers and borax until the bag is full.
5. Squeeze out the air in the bag and tie it shut.
6. Cover the coffee can and store it at room temperature for about a month.
7. Make sure you write down the date you put the flowers in and the probable date they will be dry.
8. After about a month remove the flowers. Use the paintbrush to gently brush away the borax.

■ Dried Flowers 3

[Makes 3 quarts drying material]

The sand can be used over and over. Use this method if you cannot wait for weeks to go by.

Materials

1 old baking pan, 9 by 12 by 2 inches   oven
3 quarts dry sand   newspapers
fresh flowers   soft paintbrush

Procedure

1. Cover the bottom of the baking pan with about one inch of sand.

2. Place the flowers "face up" in the sand.

3. Sift about an inch and a half of sand over the flowers. Gently poke the sand around all the petals.

4. Bake at 200° F for about 2 hours.

5. Test to see if the flowers are dry by gently pulling up one flower. Carefully bend a petal of the flower. If the petal breaks, the moisture is gone. The flowers are dry, and they should be removed from the oven. If the flower is still moist, bake 15 more minutes and then test again.

6. Remove the flowers from the sand and place on the newspapers. Let them cool for about 2 hours.

7. Carefully brush off the sand with the soft paintbrush.

■ Dried Flowers 4
[Makes 1 quart drying material]

Flowers can be dried in about a day with this method. The kitty litter can be used over and over.

Materials

1 quart kitty litter
microwave-safe container with lid

microwave oven
fresh flowers

Procedure

1. Place about an inch or so of kitty litter in the bottom of the microwave-safe container.
2. Place a few flowers on top of the kitty litter. Cover the flowers with more kitty litter.
3. Leave the lid off and place the container in the microwave. Microwave from 1 to 3 minutes, depending on the type of flower. The thicker the flower, the longer the time should be.
4. Remove the container from the microwave and place the lid on. However, the lid should fit very loosely.
5. Leave the container alone for at least 18 hours so that the flowers and kitty litter will slowly cool down and finish drying.
6. Remove the dried flowers from the container and shake off any extra kitty litter.

■ Dried Flowers 5
[Makes 3 cups, enough to dry a large bunch of flowers]

The glycerin is absorbed by the flowers and replaces the water. Glycerin can be purchased at a pharmacy.

Materials

2 cups hot water
1 cup glycerin
1 flower vase

fresh flowers
knife

Procedure

1. Combine the glycerin and hot water in the vase. Allow the mixture to cool.
2. Split the stems of the flowers with the knife and place them in the vase.
3. The flowers should be preserved in about 3 weeks.

12

Activities About Other Times and Other Cultures

Every culture has unique characteristics. However, many similarities exist among cultures. Most of the great ancient cultures flourished in warm regions with good farmland near rivers. Almost every culture developed advanced farming techniques and food storage devices. Almost every culture was concerned about the afterlife.

■ Mummifying Material
[Makes 2½ cups material]

The ancient Egyptians lived in a narrow band along the Nile River. They had to deal with sand, heat, and aridity. They built their homes from clay bricks, and they built their pyramids from stones transported hundreds of miles down the Nile. They devoted their lives to preparation for the afterlife. The ancient Egyptians were famous for their mummifying techniques. The mummification of a piece of fruit allows students to understand the mummification process. Washing soda (sodium carbonate) is located in the laundry products section of the grocery store.

Materials

1 cup baking soda
1 cup washing soda
½ cup iodized salt
1 apple or pear, cut in half

1 disposable container large enough to hold about 4 cups of material
mixing spoon

Procedure

1. Combine the baking soda, washing soda, and salt in the container.

2. Bury the apple or pear halves in the mixture.

3. Let stand for 10 days and remove the dried apple or pear.

■ Fake Papyrus
[Makes enough for 1 project]

This project requires patience and luck. The Egyptians made papyrus writing material from papyrus reeds. In fact, etymologists trace the root of the word "paper" back to papyrus.

Materials

3 stalks of rhubarb	hammer
vegetable peeler	lots of newspaper
old cookie sheet with lip	heavy weights

Procedure

1. Place several layers of newspaper on the old cookie sheet.
2. With the vegetable peeler, peel several length-wise strips of rhubarb.
3. Lay about five strips of rhubarb side by side on the newspaper.
4. Turn the cookie sheet 90 degrees. Place about five strips of rhubarb side by side on top of the first layer. The second layer should be perpendicular to the first layer.
5. Place two sheets of newspaper on top of the rhubarb.
6. Gently pound the rhubarb-newspaper layers.
7. Remove the top layer of newspapers and add a new layer of newspapers.
8. Place several heavy weights on top of the layers.
9. Over the next 2 days, replace the newspaper when moisture seeps through.
10. After 2 days remove the newspaper. The papyrus is in one sheet, and it should resemble paper.

■ Sugar Cube Pyramid

[Makes 1 pyramid]

The ancient Egyptians built huge pyramids as tombs for their pharaohs. This sugar cube pyramid is an easy way to show how pyramids were made. Students should not eat the icing because it contains raw egg white.

Materials

1 egg white
⅛ teaspoon cream of tartar
1½ cups confectioners' sugar
at least 385 sugar cubes
    (about 2 boxes)*
mixing bowl

mixing spoon
eggbeater
knife
sturdy cardboard base about 12 inches by
    12 inches
aluminum foil

*The project requires 385 sugar cubes. However, some cubes may break. Plan to have extra cubes available.

Procedure

1. Make a mortar by combining the egg white and cream of tartar in the mixing bowl.
2. Beat with the eggbeater until soft peaks form.
3. Slowly add the confectioners' sugar, small amounts at a time, until icing forms.
4. Cover the cardboard base with aluminum foil.
5. Spread a thin layer of icing on the base.
6. Place 100 cubes on the icing in 10 rows of 10 each. Place a small amount of icing between each cube before placing it next to another cube.
7. Spread a thin layer of icing on top of the first row.
8. The next layer should be made of 81 sugar cubes in 9 rows of 9 each. Remember to place a small amount of icing between cubes.
9. The next layer should be 64 sugar cubes in 8 rows of 8 each.
10. Continue each layer until the last layer has 1 cube.
11. Allow to harden before moving.

■ Rainstick
[Makes 1]

Rainsticks were created by Native Americans. Rainsticks can be purchased in stores in the American Southwest and can be very expensive. This project costs very little. The sound is very soothing.

Materials

paper towel tube or other long
    cardboard tube
small piece of cardboard or oaktag
20 small nails
scissors

masking tape
1 cup small dried beans or dried corn
markers or other items to decorate
    finished product

Procedure

1. Cut two cardboard circles the size of the openings of the tube.
2. Tape one of the circles to one end of the tube.
3. Insert the small nails at various places along the tube.
4. Pour in the small dried beans or corn.
5. Tape the other cardboard circle to the open end of the cardboard tube.
6. Decorate.
7. Turn upside down and listen to the rainstick.

■ Adobe Bricks
[Makes as many as the class wants to make]

Almost every ancient culture built structures from clay bricks dried in the sun. The southwestern Native Americans used adobe bricks to build their homes. They used adobe because they had the materials to make it. Students could experiment and make some bricks with straw or grass clippings and some without. Which ones are sturdier? Why?

Materials

soil, hopefully with a bit of clay in it
dry grass clippings or straw
water
bucket

1 half-gallon wax-carton milk container
scissors
old knife

Procedure

1. In the bucket combine equal amounts of soil and grass clippings.
2. Add enough water to make thick mud, and blend the three ingredients.
3. With the scissors, cut out one of the long sides of the milk carton.
4. Cut out its opposite side.
5. Force the triangular top down so that the milk carton is now rectangular. It is now an adobe mold.
6. Place the milk carton mold on a bed of grass clippings or straw.
7. Fill the milk carton mold with some of the adobe mixture and let stand an hour or two.
8. Use the knife to go around the edges of the mold and remove the carton.
9. Repeat with more adobe.
10. Do not move the bricks. Let them dry for several days.

■ Simple Loom

[Makes 1]

Just about every culture developed a simple loom. This loom is easy to make, cheap, and durable.

Materials

1 piece very stiff cardboard about
    5 inches by 7 inches
about 24 feet of heavy duty string
yarn

ruler
pencil
scissors
transparent tape

Procedure

1. With the ruler and pencil mark off every quarter inch along both of the 5-inch sides of the piece of cardboard. These 2 sides will become the ends of the looms.
2. Make a cut about ½ inch deep at each quarter-inch mark.
3. Decide which side of the cardboard will be the underside of the loom. On that side, tape one end of the string.
4. Wind the string around the loom and through the cuts so that about 20 parallel strings now run the length of the loom. These are warp threads.
5. Tape the end of the string to the underside of the loom.
6. Return to the top side of the loom. Cut off a piece of yarn and tie it to the extreme left string at the bottom. This is the weft.
7. Wind a small piece of tape around the other end of the weft so that the yarn will not fray.
8. Begin weaving by going over the first warp and under the next. Repeat the process until you reach the end warp thread. Then reverse directions. Continue weaving until you wish to change colors or the yarn runs out.
9. Students can make stripes or even more intricate patterns on their looms.
10. When the weaving is complete, it is time to take the completed project off the loom. Cut the strings along the underside of the loom.
11. Turn the loom over. Remove two neighboring strings from the notches and tie them together. Continue until all the strings have been removed and knotted.
12. The strings make a nice fringe for the weaving, or they can be trimmed.

■ Iyaga (Inuit Toss and Catch Toy)
[Makes 1]

Many cultures have a toy similar to the iyaga. The Inuit made their toy from bones and string.

Materials

1 unsharpened pencil
1 metal washer with a fairly wide
hole (or rubber canning ring)

1 piece of string about 18 inches long

Procedure

1. Tie one end of the string to the pencil close to the eraser.
2. Tie the other end of the string to the washer.
3. A child holds the pencil and swings the string to try to catch the washer on the pencil.
4. A variation of this game is adding more washers to the string.

■ Cascarones
[Makes 1]

In Central and South America, cascarones are gently cracked over people's heads during Carnival, the time just before Lent.

Materials

1 large egg (decorated if possible)
1 needle
small pair of scissors

2 tablespoons confetti
small piece of tissue paper
glue

Procedure

1. Use the needle to make a small hole in one end of the egg.
2. Enlarge the hole to about the size of a nickel.
3. Empty out the egg and wash and dry the shell.
4. Pour in the confetti.
5. Cover the hole with a small piece of tissue paper and glue the paper in place.
6. Allow the glue to dry.
7. Wait for Carnival and carefully crack away!

■ Paper Flowers
[Makes 6]

Paper flowers are a part of many cultures, including those of Mexico and Central America.

Materials

18 to 24 pieces of tissue paper about 6 inches by 6 inches

scissors
6 pipe cleaners

Procedure

1. Cut the tissue paper into irregular shapes.
2. Cut some large sizes, some medium sizes, and some small sizes.
3. Stack 3 or 4 pieces of tissue paper, large to small.
4. Make 2 small holes in the center of the tissue paper stack.
5. Weave a pipe cleaner through the two holes and twist the ends together to make the stem.
6. Pull the tissue pieces away from the stems to make the flower full.
7. Complete the other flowers.

13
Face and Body Paints

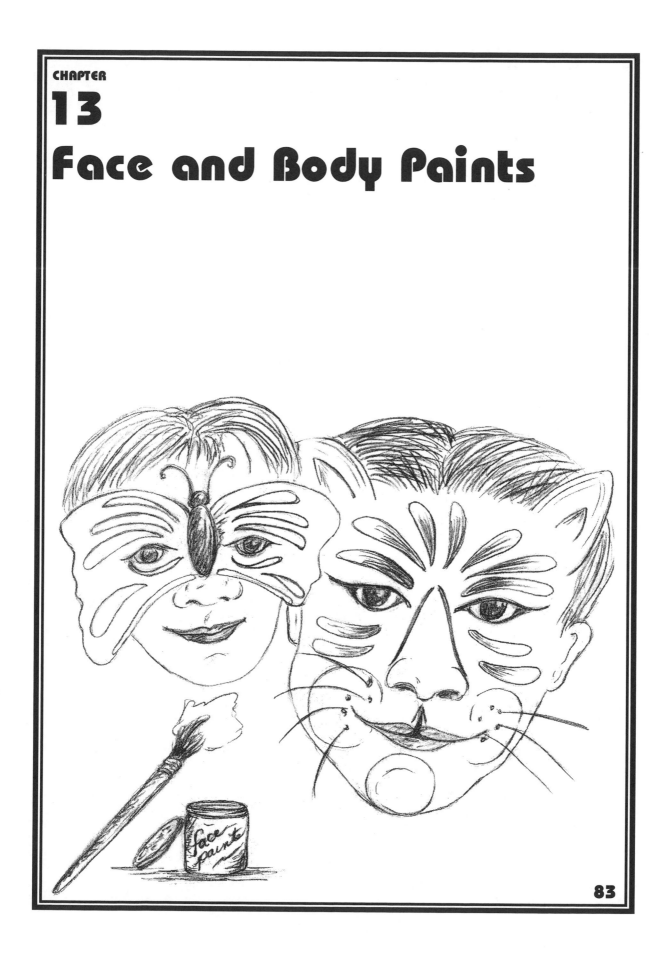

Commercial face painting kits are expensive and limited in colors. Face paints can be made with readily available ingredients and a little imagination. Remember to test these face paints on a small patch of skin before making large designs because some students could have a reaction to the materials.

■ Cornstarch Face Paint
[Makes 3 tablespoons]

Keep food coloring away from clothing.

Materials

2 tablespoons shortening
1 tablespoon cornstarch
3–6 drops food coloring
small container

mixing spoon
cotton swabs, small brushes, or make-up
    sponges

Procedure

1. Combine the shortening and cornstarch in the small container.
2. Add the food coloring until desired shade is reached.
3. Apply with cotton swabs, small brushes, or make-up sponges.
4. Remove with soap and water.

■ Body Paint
[Makes 3 tablespoons]

Cold cream can be purchased at a drugstore or cosmetics supply store. It is very thick, and it easily combines with other ingredients. Keep food coloring away from clothing.

Materials

1 tablespoon cold cream
1 tablespoon cornstarch
1 tablespoon water
3–6 drops food coloring

small container
mixing spoon
cotton swabs, small brushes, or make-up
    sponges

Procedure

1. Combine the cold cream and cornstarch in the small container.
2. Stir in the water until the mixture is creamy.
3. Add the food coloring until desired shade is reached.
4. Apply with cotton swabs, small brushes, or make-up sponges.
5. Remove with soap and water.

■ Corn Syrup Face Paint

[Makes 2 tablespoons]

This face paint can be applied easily to the face. Keep food coloring away from clothing.

Materials

1 tablespoon cold cream
1 tablespoon corn syrup
3–6 drops food coloring
small container

mixing spoon
cotton swabs, small brushes, or make-up
    sponges

Procedure

1. Combine the cold cream and corn syrup in the small container.
2. Add the food coloring until desired shade is reached.
3. Apply with cotton swabs, small brushes, or make-up sponges.
4. Remove with soap and water.

■ Baby Shampoo Face Paint

[Makes 3 tablespoons]

The tempera paint could stain clothing.

Materials

3 tablespoons baby shampoo
powdered tempera paint
small mixing bowl

mixing spoon
cotton swabs, small brushes, or make-up
    sponges

Procedure

1. Pour the baby shampoo into the small mixing bowl.
2. Add the powdered tempera paint until desired shade is reached.
3. Apply with cotton swabs, small brushes, or make-up sponges.
4. Remove with soap and water.

■ Baby Lotion Face Paint
[Makes ¼ cup]

The tempera paint could stain clothing.

Materials

¼ cup baby lotion
powdered tempera paint
2 teaspoons dish detergent
small mixing bowl

mixing spoon
cotton swabs, small brushes, or make-up
    sponges

Procedure

1. Pour the baby lotion into the small mixing bowl.

2. Add the powdered tempera paint until desired shade is reached.

3. Stir in the dish detergent.

4. Apply with cotton swabs, small brushes, or make-up sponges.

5. Remove with water.

14
Recycled Paper and Paper Projects

■ Mashed Potato Paper

[Makes enough for about 8 pieces of paper]

Herbs, pine needles, flower petals, and other small pieces of nature can be added to the pulp to give it variety and maybe even an aroma.

Materials

6 large raw potatoes	scissors
scraps of old, soft paper	large rubber band
vegetable peeler	old dishpan
grater	old newspapers
blender	old towels
large, old bowl	rolling pin
water	spray starch
clothes hanger	iron
old panty hose	

Procedure

1. Peel the potatoes and grate them in the large bowl.
2. Add scraps of paper equal in volume to the amount of grated potato.
3. Combine and cover with water. Set aside for a few hours.
4. Make a screen by first forming a square from the hanger. Then slip it into the panty hose and trim off the excess panty hose. Secure with a rubber band.
5. Using your fingers, mash up the potato-paper-water mixture.
6. Pour about a cup of the mixture into the blender. Add more water and blend until uniform.
7. Pour mixture into old dishpan and repeat with another batch of the mixture.
8. After all the mixture has been blended, dip the screen under the mixture and bring up some of the mixture.
9. Making sure the frame is level, allow most of the water to drip back into the dishpan.
10. Press down gently on the mixture to remove more of the water.
11. Place several layers of newspaper on the work surface. Place an old towel on top of the newspaper.
12. Gently flip the screen over so that the mixture is now on the old towel.
13. Cover the mixture with another old towel.
14. Use the rolling pin to roll out even more water.
15. Remove the top towel and place the mixture on a smooth surface and let dry overnight.
16. The dry paper is actually completed, but it could be made flatter by spraying lightly with starch. Then cover with a thin towel and iron at a warm setting.

■ Pinwheel
[Makes 1]

This project has been around for a very long time. A windy spring morning would be great weather for pinwheels. Students can decorate the paper before it is bent and fastened.

Materials

1 piece square construction paper
about 10 inches on each side
scissors

1 straight pin
1 pencil with a new eraser

Procedure

1. Hold a tip of the piece of paper and fold across to the opposite tip, pressing to make a crease. The shape should be a triangle.

2. Open the paper and fold so that the other two tips meet. Press to make a crease.

3. Open the paper again.

4. The center is where the two creases meet.

5. Cut along the creases, close to but not through the center. You should have 4 triangles joined at the center.

6. Take a corner of one triangle and bring it to the center. Hold it in place.

7. Do the same for the corresponding corners of the other 3 triangles.

8. Push the straight pin through the corners, through the center, and into the pencil eraser.

9. Make sure the straight pin allows the pinwheel to turn freely.

■ Vertical Spinner
[Makes 1]

This project, amazingly simple to do, produces such excitement. It lends itself to many further investigations. Can we add more paper clips? Can we shorten the wings? Can we make it from other materials? Students can devote quite a few science sessions to setting up and conducting experiments.

Materials

1 piece of stiff paper about 2 inches by 6 inches

medium size paper clip
scissors

Procedure

1. Hold the paper on one side and cut it lengthwise down the middle about 2⅓ inches.
2. About an inch below that cut, make two cuts about ¾ inch each on each side.
3. Go back to the first cut and fold one flap in one direction and the other flap in the other direction. These form the "wings" of the twirler.
4. Now go to the second cut. From one cut fold the paper lengthwise in the direction opposite that of its corresponding wing.
5. Fold the paper lengthwise from the other cut in the direction opposite that of its corresponding wing.
6. Fold up the bottom inch of the twirler and add a paper clip.
7. Hold the twirler as high as possible just under the wings and drop it. It spins as it drops.

■ Horizontal Spinner
[Makes 1]

This project also causes great excitement. Can we make it smaller? How big can we make it? Does it work without paper clips?

Materials

1 strip of construction paper, 1 inch by 7 inches

1 paper clip

Procedure

1. Fold the paper in half so that it is 1 inch by 3½ inches.
2. Approximately 1 inch from the folded end, fold down the end at a 45° angle.
3. Approximately 1 inch from the unfolded end, fold down the end at a 45° angle, but in the opposite direction from the other end.
4. Fasten the paper clip in the middle of the paper.
5. Open up the two ends slightly to form wings.
6. Drop paper and watch it spin.

■ Circular Spinner
[Makes 1]

These spinners can become quite colorful if crayons or markers are used to decorate the circle.

Materials

manila folder or piece of somewhat   compass
    stiff cardboard   scissors

Procedure

1. Use the compass to create an 8-inch circle on the manila folder.
2. Cut out the circle.
3. Cut six evenly spaced slits, each about 2½ inches long, from the edge of the circle toward the center.
4. Now fold along the slits to create flaps of about 45 degrees. Make sure the flaps all go in the same direction.
5. Hold the spinner high up but horizontal to the floor and drop it.
6. It should spin as it falls to the ground.

■ Chinese Cobweb
[Makes 1]

Make very close cuts to create an intricate cobweb.

Materials

1 large circular piece of construction   scissors
    paper or crepe paper

Procedure

1. Fold the construction or crepe paper circle in half, and in half again. Fold for a third time.
2. Alternate cutting slits along each side. Each cut should reach within an inch of the other side. Each cut should be about a half inch from the previous cut.
3. Unfold the paper and pull apart to make the cobweb.

■ Flower Cage
[Makes 1]

These cobweb cutouts are called flower cages because pictures of flowers were often hidden below the cut circles of paper.

Materials

construction paper	paper clip
compass	picture of flowers
scissors	glue
string	

Procedure

1. Use the compass to make a large circle on the construction paper. Cut it out.
2. Fold the circle in half and then in half two more times.
3. Use the scissors to make a curved cut from one fold almost to the other side.
4. Make another cut from the opposite side almost to the other fold. This cut should be about a half inch from the previous cut.
5. Continue making alternate, curved cuts until the point is reached.
6. Make a small hole at the point of the folded paper. Unfold the paper.
7. Tie the paper clip to the string and gently place the paper clip through the small hole.
8. Glue the edge of the circle onto a picture of flowers. Glue the picture onto another piece of construction paper.
9. Pull the string and watch the paper form a cage. The flowers should appear to peek out from the cage.

■ Flower Cage Garland
[Makes 1]

These flower cage garlands would be great to make during Chinese New Year.

Materials

flower cages (see previous procedure)   string
glue

Procedure

1. Place one flower cage circle on table. Put glue at four equally spaced spots on edge of the circle.
2. Place a second flower cage circle on top of it.
3. Place some glue in the middle of the second circle.
4. Place a third circle on top of the second circle.
5. Continue gluing on circles, alternating the glue locations.
6. Let the glue dry. Pull apart the circles and watch the garland unfold. Hang with string.

■ Paper Weaving
[Makes 1]

The following method produces a rectangular product. However, the weavings can be cut into Christmas decorations or even animal shapes. Just add wings or fins or feet.

Materials

two 9-inch-by-12-inch pieces of construction paper, different colors	ruler
	scissors
	glue
pencil	

Procedure

1. Fold one sheet of the construction paper in half horizontally.
2. Use the ruler and the pencil to make a 1-inch border on the 9-inch side. This is the cutting limit.
3. From the fold make cuts to the line. Each cut should be about an inch from the next cut.
4. Unfold the paper. This portion will serve as both loom and warp.
5. Cut the other piece of construction paper into strips 1 inch wide and 9 inches long. These strips will serve as weft.
6. Weave one weft strip over the first warp strip and then under the next strip and then over the next and so on.
7. Weave the next weft strip under the first warp strip and then over the next strip and under the next and so on.
8. Continue the weaving until the loom is full.
9. Glue edges of warp and weft if desired.

■ Paper Wreath or Star or Flower
[Makes 1]

The trick is in the last fold and the glue. A Christmas wreath can be made from green construction paper, and red mistletoe berries (either real or paper) can be added. A star can be made by pinching the ends. Glitter can easily be glued on. Spring flowers can also be made from smaller pieces of construction paper.

Materials

1 piece of construction paper, 12 inches by 18 inches
scissors

glue
stapler and staples

Procedure

1. Fold the paper in half horizontally so that the long ends meet.
2. Fold one long end down about an inch.
3. Fold the other long end down about an inch but in the other direction.
4. Make quite a few cuts from the middle fold to these new folds. Each new cut should be about ¾ of an inch away from the previous cut.
5. Unfold the paper and reverse the paper so that the previous inside is now the outside.
6. Lay one short edge over the other so that a tube is formed. Glue the overlapped edges together.
7. Bring the ends of the tube together to form a wreath and staple the two ends together.
8. Decorate and enjoy.

15
Growing Plants

Just about every year, every primary student grows a plant. Here are some easy ways to make plants an important part of the classroom.

■ Sweet Potato Plant
[Makes 1 plant]

The sweet potato vine can become quite long. Students could incorporate some math into the activity by charting its weekly growth.

Materials

1 sweet potato	1 tall, clear plastic glass
4 toothpicks	water

Procedure

1. Hold the sweet potato so that the pointed ends are vertical. Poke the 4 toothpicks into the sweet potato on all four sides at the middle.

2. Fill the plastic glass with water.

3. Place one pointed end of the sweet potato into the water so that the 4 toothpicks rest on the edge of the glass. The toothpicks keep the top half of the sweet potato out of the water. The top half should remain dry, and the bottom half should be submerged in water.

4. Place the glass in a sunny spot and wait. Add water as needed.

5. In about a week roots will grow from the bottom, and leaves will appear from the top.

6. When the sweet potato develops vines, transplant the plant to a pot filled with soil.

■ Potato Plant
[Makes about 5 plants, depending on the potato]

Students could find out what part of the plant the actual potato is.

Materials

1 potato with plenty of eyes	knife
5 hot beverage cups	aluminum tray
potting soil	

Procedure

1. Cut the potato into pieces so that each piece has at least one eye.
2. Use the knife to cut a small hole in the bottom of each cup so that extra water can drain out.
3. Pour enough potting soil into each cup to form a layer about an inch thick.
4. Place a piece of the potato in each cup and fill with more potting soil to near the top of the cup.
5. Place the cups on the aluminum tray and water them. Make sure the soon-to-be plants get plenty of sun.
6. The new plants should appear within a few days.

■ Carrot Plant
[Makes 1 plant]

The green leaves are the key to this project. Are we cloning the carrot?

Materials

1 carrot with green leaves and stems	water
1 aluminum pie pan	

Procedure

1. Cut off the top of the carrot so that about an inch of the carrot is still attached to the stem and leaves.
2. Place the top in a pan of water so that the stem and leaves are upright. Keep adding water as it evaporates.
3. The new plant should begin to grow in about a week.

■ Pineapple Plant
[Makes 1 plant]

Is the pineapple part that we eat a fruit? Is it a stem? Is it a sort of leaf?

Materials

1 pineapple with green leaves and
  stems
1 aluminum pie pan

soil
water

Procedure

1. Cut off the top of the pineapple so that about an inch of the fruit is still attached to the stem and leaves.

2. Pour about an inch of soil into the aluminum pie pan.

3. Place the top of the pineapple into the pan of soil. Moisten and keep adding water as it evaporates.

4. The new plant should begin to grow in about a week.

■ Avocado Plant
[Makes 1 plant]

Students could investigate the nutritional value of the avocado. They could make some guacamole from the flesh of the avocado.

Materials

1 avocado pit
4 toothpicks

1 tall, clear plastic glass
water

Procedure

1. Hold the pit so that the base is down. Poke the 4 toothpicks into the avocado pit on all four sides at the middle.

2. Fill the plastic glass with water.

3. Place the avocado pit in the water so that the 4 toothpicks rest on the edge of the glass. The toothpicks keep the top half out of the water. The top half of the pit should remain dry, and the base should be submerged in water.

4. Place the glass in a sunny spot and wait. Add water as needed.

5. In about a week roots will grow from the bottom, and leaves will appear from the top.

6. When the avocado develops roots, transplant the plant to a pot filled with soil.

7. When the plant is about 8 inches tall, cut off the top half. This promotes development of new branches.

■ Ginger Plant
[Makes 1 plant]

Ginger root can be purchased from the produce section of a grocery store. Fresh ginger is used quite a bit in Asian cooking and medicine.

Materials

1 piece of ginger root about 3 inches long	potting soil
1 small pot and saucer	trowel

Procedure

1. Place about 1 inch of potting soil in the small pot.
2. Place one end of the ginger root into the soil and surround the root with more potting soil.
3. Make sure part of the root is above the soil.
4. Water and place in direct sunlight. A plant should appear within 2 weeks.

■ Plants from Seeds
[Makes enough for 1 experiment]

Students can watch the development of the root system in this activity.

Materials

1 large plastic cup	paper towels
seeds (lima bean or radish seeds are good)	water

Procedure

1. Line the plastic cup with paper towels.
2. Pour about an inch of water into the cup.
3. Place the seeds between the inside of the plastic cup and the paper towels.
4. Place the plastic cup in a sunny place. Be sure to keep water in the bottom of the cup.
5. In about a week the seeds should germinate.
6. Transplant the seeds to pots with soil, or plant outside.

■ Grass Head

[Makes 1 head]

Students can chart the growth of the grass. They can pull out some of the grass and examine the roots under a hand lens.

Materials

1 hot beverage cup   grass seeds
colored markers   water
potting soil

Procedure

1. The cup will be the head, so a face can be drawn on the cup with markers.
2. Fill the cup about ⅔ full with potting soil.
3. Scatter grass seeds over the surface of the potting soil.
4. Cover the seeds with a small amount of soil.
5. Moisten the soil with water and set the cup in the sun.
6. After several days grass will appear as "hair."
7. Students can trim the grass "hair" with scissors.

■ Plants Without Soil

[Makes 1 experiment]

Hydroponics is the term for growing plants without soil. Students could research whether fruits and vegetables can be grown without soil.

Materials

1 sponge   mustard seeds
scissors   plastic wrap
water   spray bottle
aluminum tray or other device to
    catch extra water

Procedure

1. Cut the sponge into an interesting shape.
2. Soak the sponge in the water and then wring it out. The sponge should be moist but not dripping.
3. Place the sponge in the aluminum tray.
4. Sprinkle mustard seeds on the top of the sponge.
5. Place the tray in a sunny spot.
6. At night cover the tray with plastic wrap.
7. Fill the spray bottle with water and mist the sponge as needed to keep it moist.
8. Within 2 weeks sprouts should appear.

■ Root Systems With and Without Soil
[Makes 1 set]

Students could see if the seeds without soil sprout at the same time as the seeds with soil.

Materials

empty, clear plastic jar
sponge cut to closely fit the bottom of
   the jar
water

lima bean seeds
paper cup
potting soil

Procedure

1. Moisten the sponge and put it on the bottom of the jar.
2. Carefully arrange some lima bean seeds between the side of the jar and the sponge.
3. Pour some of the potting soil into the paper cup.
4. Plant some lima bean seeds in the soil.
5. Moisten the soil.
6. Keep both the sponge and the potting soil damp.
7. Place both of them in a sunny spot.
8. Record the sprouting roots and leaves.

■ Miniature Terrarium
[Makes 1 plant]

Some bags could be left open, and others could be closed. Is the rate of germination the same?

Materials

zip-closed plastic bag
½ cup soil

about 10 popcorn kernels
water

Procedure

1. Pour the soil into the bag.
2. Place about 10 popcorn kernels in the soil.
3. Add a small amount of water and close the bag.
4. Place in a sunny area. Within about a week roots should appear.

16
Science Projects

■ Anemometer
[Makes 1]

An anemometer measures wind speed. The faster the marked cup spins, the stronger the wind.

Materials

1 wood block about 5 inches by
    5 inches by 2 inches
2 long nails
1 drinking straw
1 paper plate

3 small paper cups
3 brass paper fasteners
hammer
hole punch

Procedure

1. Drive one nail through the bottom of the wood block to form a base.

2. Place the drinking straw over the end of the nail and stand the base on a table.

3. Center the paper plate over the straw and poke the other nail through the plate and into the straw's hole. This should anchor the plate to the straw, but the plate should be able to spin.

4. Place the three paper cups on their sides on the plate so that they form an equilateral triangle. The lip of one cup should be close to the bottom of the cup ahead of it.

5. Attach the paper cups to the plate with the brass paper fasteners.

6. Make a mark on one of the cups.

7. Take the anemometer outside on a breezy day. Place the anemometer on a steady surface away from buildings. Allow the anemometer to spin, and count the number of times the marked cup rotates in 10 seconds.

■ Weather Vane
[Makes 1]

A weather vane measures wind direction.

Materials

1 wood block about 5 inches by 5 inches by 2 inches
2 long nails
1 drinking straw

1 piece of oaktag about 6 inches by 6 inches
glue
hammer

Procedure

1. Drive 1 nail through the bottom of the wood block to form a base.

2. Place the drinking straw over the end of the nail and stand the base on a table.

3. Cut two arrows from the oaktag. Each arrow should be about 6 inches by 2 inches.

4. Make a "sandwich" of the two arrows and place the other nail between them. Make sure the nail is both centered between them and perpendicular to them. Glue the arrows to the nail so that when the nail turns, the arrows move.

5. Place the nail in the straw. The arrows should be able to swing freely on the base.

■ Thermometer
[Makes 1]

A homemade thermometer is not always successful, so be patient and flexible. Consider keeping a real thermometer nearby to see if the homemade version is at least rising or falling appropriately.

Materials

1 small, empty plastic soda bottle
enough water to fill the bottle
3–4 drops food coloring
drinking straw

small wad of clay
bucket
hot water

Procedure

1. Fill the plastic soda bottle with water.

2. Add the food coloring so that the liquid can be made more visible.

3. Place some clay around the edge of the bottle opening.

4. Place some more clay around the middle of the straw.

5. Put the straw into the bottle and squeeze the clay together so that an airtight seal has been formed.

6. Place the bottle in the bucket and pour in some hot water. The water inside the bottle should expand, and some water should rise in the straw.

■ Ocean in a Bottle

[Makes 1]

The "ocean" is caused by the fact that oil and water do not mix. Mineral oil can be purchased at a pharmacy.

Materials

1 clear plastic 1-liter bottle with lid
1½ cups mineral oil
small bowl

water
several drops blue food coloring
masking tape

Procedure

1. Pour the mineral oil into the bottle.
2. In the bowl mix the water and blue food coloring.
3. Pour enough blue water into the bottle to fill it.
4. Screw on the lid and seal with tape.
5. Turn the bottle on its side and rock gently to watch the "ocean."

■ Miniature Tornado

[Makes 1]

Students could find out how real tornadoes are generated. They could also find out what parts of the country get more tornadoes than other parts.

Materials

1 plastic soda bottle with a cap
   (16 ounces is best)
enough water to fill the bottle

4 drops liquid dish detergent
2 teaspoons glitter or plastic confetti

Procedure

1. Fill the bottle with cold water.
2. Add the liquid dish detergent and the glitter.
3. Screw on the cap.
4. Hold the bottle upside down by the neck. Rotate the bottle quickly about 5 times in a clockwise motion. Stop and watch the miniature tornado in action inside the bottle.

■ Exothermic Reaction: Instant Heat

[Makes 1 experiment]

Hand warmers can be purchased, and they have all the ingredients in this formula. When the ingredients are exposed to air, a chemical reaction occurs and heat is a by-product. The iron is the fuel. The salt and activated charcoal help the iron react quickly with oxygen in the air. The water mixes up all the chemicals. The vermiculite keeps the water within the chemicals, and the pencil shavings contain the heat.

Materials

2 teaspoons salt

2½ tablespoons vermiculite (can be purchased from a hardware store or plant nursery)

2 tablespoons iron powder (can be purchased from science catalog)

2 tablespoons fine activated charcoal (the kind used in aquarium filters)

3½ tablespoons pencil sharpener shavings

2 tablespoons water

1 small, disposable container

1 disposable spoon

Procedure

1. Combine the dry ingredients in the small, disposable container.

2. Add the water and mix.

3. The oxygen in the air will combine with the ingredients to produce heat. Students can feel the heat by touching the container.

■ Camera
[Makes 1 camera]

The image should be upside down in this camera.

Materials

1 round, empty oatmeal box without lid
scissors
1 piece of aluminum foil about 3 inches by 3 inches

1 pin
1 sheet white tissue paper
masking tape
a small light source
dark room

Procedure

1. Use the scissors to cut a hole about a ½ inch across in the bottom of the oatmeal box.

2. Cover the hole with the aluminum foil and secure with masking tape. The aluminum foil's shiny side should face the oatmeal box.

3. Make a small hole in the center of the aluminum foil with the pin.

4. Cover the open end of the box with a layer of tissue paper and secure with masking tape.

5. Turn on the small light source in the dark room. Point the pinhole toward the light. The small light source should be projected upside down on the tissue paper. You may have to move toward or away from the light source to focus the image.

■ Cloud 1
[Makes 1 cloud]

Students could investigate how real clouds form.

Materials

empty, clear plastic 2-liter soda bottle with cap
1 cup water
5 drops food coloring

match
flashlight
dark room

Procedure

1. Pour the water into the soda bottle and add the food coloring.

2. Light the match, blow it out, and immediately drop it into the soda bottle. Cap it.

3. Squeeze the bottle several times.

4. Take the bottle into the dark room and shine the flashlight through the side of the bottle. You should see a cloud.

■ Cloud 2

[Makes 1]

Students can learn about the different kinds of clouds. They can observe the weather and make a daily chart of the clouds. Students should be careful around the very hot water.

Materials

3 cups very hot water
clear glass measuring cup
old pair of panty hose

rubber band
10 ice cubes

Procedure

1. Pour the hot water into the measuring cup.
2. Carefully touch the side of the measuring cup. When it becomes fairly hot, pour out all but about ½ cup of the water.
3. Stretch one section of the panty hose over the top of the measuring cup.
4. Fasten the rubber band around the panty hose and the top of the measuring cup.
5. Place the ice cubes on top of the panty hose.
6. Water vapor inside the cup will form small clouds.

■ Sunset

[Makes 1]

The flashlight acts as the sun. The water is earth's atmosphere, and the milk is earth's air pollution. The light from the flashlight bounces around in the jar, and many of the colors of the spectrum are absorbed by the tiny suspended droplets of milk. But the red light passes through the suspended droplets of milk, so a red sunset is seen.

Materials

small glass jar with lid
about 10 drops of whole milk
water

flashlight
dark room

Procedure

1. Fill the jar almost to the top with the water.
2. Add the milk.
3. Screw on the lid and shake well.
4. Take the jar and flashlight to the dark room.
5. Shine the flashlight through one side of the jar. Look on the opposite side of the jar. A red sunset should appear.

■ Easy Prism
[Makes 1]

A prism breaks up visible light into its various parts.

Materials

jar
water

mirror small enough to fit into jar
white paper

Procedure

1. Fill the jar with water.
2. Place the mirror in the jar so that it sits at an angle.
3. Turn the jar so that the mirror faces the sun.
4. Hold the paper at an angle in front of the mirror. Move the paper until the bands of color become distinct.

■ Amazing Water: Demonstration of Adhesion and Cohesion
[Makes 1 demonstration]

This experiment works because of adhesion and cohesion. Water molecules like to stick to each other (cohesion). Water molecules also like to cling to other substances (adhesion). Students might want to practice this outside until they become good at it.

Materials

large measuring cup with pouring
    spout
another smaller glass container

water
several drops food coloring
piece of string about 36 inches long

Procedure

1. Fill the measuring cup with water.
2. Add enough food coloring to make the liquid very visible.
3. Soak the string for about 30 seconds in the water.
4. Tie one end of the string to the measuring cup handle and lay the string across the spout.
5. Place the other end of the string in the smaller glass container.
6. Hold the measuring cup in one hand and the string in the smaller glass container with the other hand.
7. Stretch the string as far as it will go and raise the measuring cup about 1 foot higher than the smaller glass container.
8. Slowly pour the liquid from the measuring cup.
9. The liquid should follow along the string and fill the smaller glass container. This takes some practice.

■ Layers of Liquid 1

[Makes 1]

Students could hypothesize about why this demonstration works. What would happen if they prepared another jar and put the honey in last?

Materials

½ cup honey or syrup   clear plastic pint jar
½ cup water   small bowl
several drops red food coloring   spoon
½ cup cooking oil

Procedure

1. Pour the honey into the jar.

2. Combine the food coloring and water in the small bowl.

3. Pour the food coloring/water mixture slowly on top of the honey. To slow down the pouring, place the spoon in the jar and trickle the water against the back of the spoon. The water should stay on top of the honey.

4. Slowly trickle the cooking oil on top of the water.

■ Layers of Liquid 2

[Makes 1]

Students could experiment with the food coloring. Will the rubbing alcohol accept the color?

Materials

½ cup water   clear plastic pint jar
several drops red food coloring   small bowl
½ cup rubbing alcohol*   spoon

*Rubbing alcohol should not be consumed.

Procedure

1. Combine the water and food coloring in the small bowl. Pour the mixture into the jar.

2. Carefully pour the rubbing alcohol on top of the water. The two layers should not mix.

■ Permanent Magnet
[Makes 1]

This project requires patience. The magnet will not be very strong.

Materials

1 stainless steel needle   paperclips
1 strong bar magnet

Procedure

1. Stroke the stainless steel needle in one direction about 250 times with the bar magnet. The needle will be magnetized.

2. Try the new magnet out by placing it near a paperclip. What happens?

■ Compass
[Makes 1]

Orienteering is navigating between the checkpoints on an outdoor course by using a compass. Students could make a compass good enough to use in orienteering and even create their own orienteering course.

Materials

3 needles   thread
bar magnet   pencil
index card   tape
scissors   jar with wide mouth

Procedure

1. Rub 2 needles about 250 times in the same direction, from the eye to the point, with the north pole of the magnet. Both needles are now magnets.

2. Cut the index card to a size 2 inches by 3 inches and fold lengthwise.

3. Unfold the index card. Tape a needle to each inside fold. Make sure the needles are parallel. Both points should face the same direction.

4. Refold the card.

5. Thread the third needle and poke through the middle of the fold from inside. Tie off the thread and leave at least 4 inches of thread free. Cut the needle off the thread.

6. Tie the end of the thread around the middle of a pencil so that the card swings freely.

7. Place the card inside the jar and suspend the pencil across the top of the jar.

8. The card should rotate until it points north-south.

9. This magnet is temporary. Eventually the needles will lose their magnetism.

■ Periscope
[Makes 1]

Submariners and spies use periscopes. Students could try to make telescoping periscopes, ones whose length can change.

Materials

2 clean, empty half-gallon wax-carton
    milk containers
scissors

2 small mirrors
2 pieces of cardboard
tape

Procedure

1. Cut the tops off the milk cartons.
2. Trim one piece of cardboard so that it will fit into the milk carton.
3. Tape a small mirror onto the cardboard.
4. Place the piece of cardboard with mirror facing out so that one edge rests on the carton's bottom and the opposite edge rests on the carton's side at a 45° angle to the bottom. Tape the piece of cardboard in place.
5. Cut a small square away from the milk carton on the side opposite the one that the cardboard rests on.
6. Repeat steps 2 through 5 with the other milk carton, cardboard, and mirror.
7. Join the two milk cartons together at their open ends. Make sure the mirrors are parallel to each other.
8. Tuck one carton slightly into the other so that they are fastened together. Tape the two milk cartons together.
9. Now face a door or other object. Look through one small opening of the periscope. Can you see the door or object? If so, the periscope is a success. If not, the mirrors may need to be adjusted.
10. See if the periscope can see around corners.

■ Screaming Cup
[Makes 1]

The terrible sound is caused by the rough surface of the dental floss making contact with your fingers. This causes the floss to vibrate, and the cup acts as a megaphone.

Materials

1 paper cup
1 toothpick

1 piece of ribbon dental floss, 25 inches long

Procedure

1. Use the toothpick to punch a hole through the bottom of the cup.
2. Thread the ribbon dental floss through the hole.
3. Tie the end of the dental floss around the middle of the toothpick. The toothpick should be outside the cup's bottom.
4. Hold the cup in one hand. Pinch the dental floss between two fingers of your other hand. Pull on the dental floss, allowing it to slip between your fingers. This should make a terrible sound.
5. Eventually the wax on the dental floss will become smooth, and there will be no terrible sound. Simply replace the dental floss to bring back the sound.

■ Simple Telephone
[Makes 1 set]

Students could see whether these phones work if the string goes around corners. Could they add more lines to the phones?

Materials

2 paper or plastic cups
10 feet of heavy-duty string

scissors

Procedure

1. With the scissors punch a small hole in the bottom of each cup.
2. Push one end of the string through the hole, from the outside of the bottom into the cup.
3. Tie a knot in the string inside the cup so that it cannot slip out of the bottom of the cup.
4. Do the same for the other cup.
5. Now the string connects both cups—the telephones.
6. Pull the string tight.
7. One child should talk into the cup, and the other child should listen. Then they can change roles.

17
Snow Globes

Snow globes have been around for many years. Students can make snow globes as gifts. Large baby food jars are just about the right size for this project. Students can root through their own toy chests for the toys or figures. Even plastic dinosaurs can be added. Make sure the toys or figures that go inside the snow globes are not made of metal. They would rust in the water. The distilled water helps keep mold away. Consider adding a bit of antiseptic mouthwash to each jar to keep down the growth of microbes.

■ Snow Globe 1
[Makes 1]

The corn syrup allows the glitter to drift down slowly.

Materials

1 small, clear jar with tight-fitting lid	clear corn syrup
1 small toy or figure	glitter or plastic confetti
tacky glue (waterproof)	

Procedure

1. Glue the figure or toy to the inside of the lid with tacky glue. Let dry overnight.
2. Fill the jar almost to the top with corn syrup.
3. Add the glitter or plastic confetti.
4. Spread glue around the top of the jar.
5. Screw the lid on and let the glue dry.

■ Snow Globe 2
[Makes 1]

The glycerin changes the water slightly so that the glitter drifts down more slowly. Glycerin can be purchased at a pharmacy.

Materials

1 small, clear jar with tight-fitting lid	distilled water
1 small toy or figure	several drops of glycerin
tacky glue (waterproof)	glitter or plastic confetti

Procedure

1. Glue the figure or toy to the inside of the lid with tacky glue. Let dry overnight.
2. Fill the jar almost to the top with distilled water. Add several drops of glycerin.
3. Add the glitter or plastic confetti.
4. Spread glue around the top of the jar.
5. Screw the lid on and let the glue dry.

■ Snow Globe 3
[Makes 1]

Moth flakes are added to wool garments to keep moths away. Students could speculate as to the composition of moth flakes and why they do not dissolve in the distilled water.

Materials

1 small, clear jar with tight-fitting lid   distilled water
1 small toy or figure   2 teaspoons moth flakes
tacky glue (waterproof)

Procedure

1. Glue the figure or toy to the inside of the lid with tacky glue. Let dry overnight.
2. Fill the jar almost to the top with distilled water.
3. Add the moth flakes.
4. Spread glue around the top of the jar.
5. Screw the lid on and let the glue dry.

■ Snow Globe 4
[Makes 1]

The crayon shavings are brightly colored. That adds lots of interest to a snow globe.

Materials

1 small, clear jar with tight-fitting lid   baby oil
1 small toy or figure   crayon shavings
tacky glue (waterproof)

Procedure

1. Glue the figure or toy to the inside of the lid with tacky glue. Let dry overnight.
2. Fill the jar almost to the top with baby oil.
3. Add the crayon shavings.
4. Spread glue around the top of the jar.
5. Screw the lid on and let the glue dry.

18
Geology Fun

Learning about rocks can be fun and interesting. Most of these activities let students make rocks and then eat them! Only the space rocks activity does not produce an edible product.

■ Conglomerate Cookies
[Makes 36 cookies]

Make sure no one is allergic to nuts because this recipe uses peanut butter. Conglomerate rocks are composed of small pieces of mineral combined through heat or by a cement-like substance. In this demonstration the sprinkles represent the smaller pieces and the peanut butter is the cement.

Materials

¼ cup shortening
¼ cup butter
½ cup peanut butter
½ cup sugar
½ cup brown sugar, packed
1 egg
1¼ cups flour
¾ teaspoon baking powder
¾ teaspoon baking soda

¼ teaspoon salt
lots of sprinkles
shortening to grease cookie sheets
mixing bowl
mixing spoon
wax paper
cookie sheets
fork

Procedure

1. Combine the shortening, butter, peanut butter, sugar, brown sugar, and egg in the mixing bowl.
2. Add a portion of the flour and combine.
3. Add the baking powder, baking soda, and salt. Combine.
4. Add the rest of the flour and combine.
5. Cover the bowl with wax paper and refrigerate for 2 hours.
6. Remove from refrigerator and roll pieces of dough the size of large marbles.
7. Roll the balls in the sprinkles so that the balls are covered in sprinkles.
8. Grease the cookie sheets.
9. Place balls of sprinkle-covered dough 3 inches apart on the cookie sheets.
10. Flatten with fork tines.
11. Bake at 375° F for 10 to 12 minutes or until the edges become a bit brown.

■ Volcanic Candy
[Makes about 24 pieces]

Regular chocolate could be substituted for the white chocolate. The red food coloring would then be unnecessary.

Materials

2 packages white chocolate
  (6 squares each)
red food coloring
microwave-safe bowl

mixing spoon
wax paper
tray or cookie sheet

Procedure

1. Melt the white chocolate in the microwave-safe bowl (about 3 minutes).

2. Add food coloring to melted white chocolate.

3. Place wax paper on tray or cookie sheet.

4. Drop mixture by spoonfuls onto wax paper.

5. Let harden—and eat!

■ Edible Conglomerate Rocks
[Makes about 24 rocks]

Students are making crisped rice treats with a twist. The raisins, chocolate chips, and nuts represent rocks that were forced together.

Materials

80 large marshmallows
7 tablespoons butter
12 cups crisped rice cereal
8 cups raisins, chocolate chips, nuts,
  or any combination of these
  ingredients

large microwave-safe container
spoon
cooking spray
small piece of wax paper for each student

Procedure

1. Combine the marshmallows and butter in the microwave-safe container. Microwave until marshmallows have melted.

2. Stir in the crisped rice cereal.

3. Coat students' hands with cooking spray.

4. Give each child a small amount of the crisped rice cereal mixture.

5. Student can then choose from the nuts and other ingredients to add to their mixture. These ingredients are pressed into the mixture to form the conglomerate rock.

6. Let "rocks" cool on wax paper before eating.

■ Sedimentary Layer Cake
[Makes about 10 slices of cake]

Sedimentary rocks form as layers. Three-fourths of the earth's rock is sedimentary. This recipe allows students to see the layers. Students could add some sprinkles to the layers after the frosting has been applied.

Materials

1 cake mix and the extra ingredients   mixer
    the mix requires   dental floss
2 containers of frosting   cake plate
baking pans   paper plates and plastic forks

Procedure

1. Prepare the cake according to the box's instructions. Allow each of the two layers to cool.
2. Remove the layers from the pans and place on a work surface.
3. Cut each layer in half horizontally by using the dental floss as a saw.
4. Place the first layer on the plate and spread on some frosting.
5. Use the frosting to "glue" all the layers together.
6. After the first piece is cut and removed, students can see the 4 layers of cake and the 4 layers of frosting.

■ Space Rocks
[Makes 10]

Students could make these rocks and then create dioramas of the moon. They could color the liquid mixture red and make Mars rocks. Students could find out why they cannot make Jupiter or Saturn rocks. Students could also note the heat generated by the plaster of paris and water.

Materials

3 cups plaster of paris   water
10 resealable plastic bags   hammer

Procedure

1. Pour some plaster of paris into each bag.
2. Add enough water to make a thick paste.
3. Seal the bags and squish them so that the water and plaster of paris become thoroughly mixed.
4. Once the plaster of paris is hard, hit each bag with a hammer to break the solid into rocks.

19
Making Musical Instruments

Most musical instruments create sound by blowing through a tube (a trumpet), vibrating strings (a violin) or hitting something (a drum). Students learn a great deal about music when they make their own instruments, and they also learn about the science of sound.

■ Water Glass Musical Instruments
[Makes 1 set]

Students could note that the more water in a glass, the lower the sound.

Materials

8 glasses, each at least 6 inches tall
ruler

water
metal spoon

Procedure

1. Line up the 8 glasses.
2. Fill the first glass to the top with water. This will make the low C note.
3. Use the ruler to fill the next glass 8/9 full. This will make the D note.
4. Use the ruler to fill the next glass 4/5 full. This will make the E note.
5. Use the ruler to fill the next glass ¾ full. This will make the F note.
6. Use the ruler to fill the next glass ⅔ full. This will make the G note.
7. Use the ruler to fill the next glass 3/5 full. This will make the A note.
8. Use the ruler to fill the next glass 8/15 full. This will make the B note.
9. Use the ruler to fill the last glass half full. This will make the high C note.
10. Gently tap each glass with the metal spoon and begin to make music.

■ Kazoo
[Makes 1]

Music is created when the humming causes the wax paper to vibrate.

Materials

1 cardboard tube from paper towels
1 sheet wax paper about 8 inches by
    8 inches

1 rubber band
1 sharpened pencil

Procedure

1. Place the wax paper over one end of the tube and fasten with the rubber band.
2. With the pencil point make a small puncture about 2 inches from the other end of the kazoo.
3. To play, hum through the open end of the kazoo. See what happens when the hole is covered.

■ Drums
[Makes 1 set]

Just about every culture has created drums. Students could research particular types of drums.

Materials

empty oatmeal cartons or empty
    coffee cans with lids

2 pencils
masking tape

Procedure

1. Wrap enough masking tape around one end of each pencil so that small balls are formed. These become the heads of the drumsticks.
2. The oatmeal cartons or coffee cans become the drums.
3. Hit the oatmeal cartons or coffee cans with the drumsticks.
4. Can different pitches be created?

■ Tambourine
[Makes 2]

Students could try different fillings inside the paper plates. Can different sounds be made? Students could also decorate the plates.

Materials

4 paper plates
about ½ cup dried large beans,
    beads, or uncooked pasta.

stapler and staples
masking tape

Procedure

1. Place 2 plates on the table.
2. Pour about ¼ cup beans, beads, or uncooked pasta into each plate.
3. Cover each plate with another plate so that the rims touch.
4. Staple the sets of plates together.
5. Completely seal the edges together with tape.
6. Shake or hit tambourines to make music.

■ Wood Stick Tambourine

[Makes 1]

The number of bottle caps can be changed.

Materials

1 strip of wood about 2 inches by
    2 inches by 9 inches
12 bottle caps

4 nails with wide heads, about 3 inches
    long
hammer

Procedure

1. Make 4 stacks of bottle caps.
2. Place each stack on the strip of wood so that each stack is about ½ inch away from the next stack.
3. Hammer a nail through each stack so that the bottle caps are loosely fastened to the wood. They should be able to move along the length of the nail.
4. Play the wood stick tambourine by shaking it or by gently hitting it with your hand.

■ Rubber Band Guitar

[Makes 1]

The frame for the rubber bands must be very sturdy. Students can investigate how different rubber bands can produce different pitches.

Materials

1 square metal tin about 6 inches by
    6 inches (no lid is necessary)

about 6 big rubber bands of varying
    widths

Procedure

1. Place the rubber bands around the metal tin so that they stretch across the open top. Make sure the rubber bands are parallel to each other.
2. Twang away!

■ Panpipes
[Makes 1 set]

Many cultures, from ancient Egypt to present-day Peru, use versions of panpipes.

Materials

about 40 inches PVC pipe, ½ inch in
diameter
2 craft sticks*
duct tape

hacksaw
sandpaper
5 corks that will fit the ½-inch PVC pipe

*Craft sticks, also known as popsicle sticks, can be purchased at craft stores.

Procedure

1. Cut 5 lengths of pipe so that each pipe will play one note. The following list shows the lengths to be cut and the corresponding notes that can be played:
   G: 9½ inches
   A: 8½ inches
   B: 7½ inches
   D: 7 inches
   E: 6 inches

2. Sandpaper the edges so that they are not sharp.

3. Line up the 5 pieces side by side, from large to small, so that the tops are in a straight line.

4. Sandwich the tops between 2 craft sticks and bind together tightly with duct tape.

5. Place the corks in the bottom ends of the panpipes.

6. Play the panpipes by blowing across the tops of the tubes.

7. Adjust the pitch of each pipe by slightly raising or lowering the cork.

■ Boom Pipes
[Makes 1 set]

These pipes provide a wonderful, resonant sound. They can be played inside or outside. PVC pipe usually comes in 10-foot lengths.

Materials

6 lengths of 4″ PVC thin-wall drain pipe
14 end caps for the PVC pipe
14 carpet squares
hacksaw

Procedure

1. Cut 14 lengths of pipe so that each pipe will play 1 note. The following list shows the lengths to be cut and the corresponding notes that can be played.
   E: 19 inches
   D: 22 inches
   C: 24¾ inches
   B: 26¼ inches
   A: 29½ inches
   G: 33½ inches
   F sharp: 35½ inches
   F: 37 inches
   E: 40½ inches
   D: 45 inches
   C: 50½ inches
   B: 55 inches
   A: 61 inches
   G: 68¼ inches

2. Cover one end of each pipe with an end cap.

3. Play the pipes by banging a pipe (end cap down) against a carpet square.

4. If a pipe is a bit flat, cut off ¼ inch.

5. If the pipe is too sharp, add a bit of water.

■ Sand Blocks

[Makes 1 set]

Different grades of sandpaper can make different sounds. This could lead to some fun experiments.

Materials

2 blocks of wood about 5 inches by
    5 inches by 2 inches
sandpaper
scissors

thumbtacks
2 empty spools
glue

Procedure

1. Cut a piece of sandpaper so that it covers the bottom and two sides of one of the blocks.
2. Thumbtack the sandpaper to the block on two sides.
3. Repeat the procedure with the other block.
4. Glue the spools to the sides of the blocks without the sandpaper.
5. Allow the glue to dry.
6. Play the sand blocks by brushing them against one another.

■ Steel Drums

[Makes 1 set]

Real steel drums are made from oil drums that are pounded and tuned. They are popular in the Caribbean region. Empty food tins have been substituted for the steel drums. Small tins make high notes, and big tins make low notes.

Materials

3 empty, clean food tins (cookie or
    popcorn tins work well)

2 unsharpened pencils
about 6 rubber bands

Procedure

1. The empty food tins become the drums. The tins could be painted or covered with pretty decorations.
2. Wrap the rubber bands around the unsharpened pencils to make the drumsticks.
3. Have a good time!

20
Colonial Times Projects

In 1776 about 96 percent of adults were farmers. Today about 4 percent of adults are farmers. Our society has certainly become very specialized, and daily life is very different from that of the colonial period. Hopefully these activities will help students see how colonial people lived.

■ Cornhusk Doll
[Makes 1 doll]

Children had to make their own toys, even their dolls. Today's children can see how easy it is to make dolls. Cornhusks can be obtained from craft catalogs, local corn farmers, or grocery stores.

Materials

12 cornhusks	scissors
container of warm water	cotton balls
thin string or embroidery floss	

Procedure

1. Soak the cornhusks in warm water for about half an hour to make them pliable.
2. Tie the 12 husks together at the top with a length of string or embroidery floss.
3. Make the head by making another tie a bit down the husks. Fill the husks with cotton balls to fill out the head.
4. Pull away 3 husks to form an arm. Tie them together.
5. Do the same for the other arm.
6. Make the body by tying together the remaining husks about halfway down.
7. Create a leg by taking 3 of those husks and tying them together just above the ends.
8. Do the same for the other leg.
9. Add cotton ball stuffing if necessary.
10. Trim the arms if necessary to make the body proportional.
11. Make clothing from scraps of cloth if desired.

■ Cornhusk Wreath
[Makes 1]

This wreath is easy to make. The difficult part is getting the hang of knotting the cornhusks.

Materials

piece of wire about 24 inches long
pliers
about 30 cornhusks
pan of warm water

masking tape
scissors
ribbon bow, pinecones, or other
    decorations

Procedure

1. Soak the cornhusks in the pan of warm water for about half an hour to make them pliable.
2. Shape the piece of wire into a circle. Twist the ends together with the pliers.
3. Cover the area where the ends meet with masking tape.
4. Remove the cornhusks and fold each in half to make a loop.
5. Lay each folded cornhusk under the wire. Pull the tails of the husk over the wire and through the loop. Secure each knot.
6. Continue knotting on cornhusks until the wreath is full.
7. Add ribbon, pinecones, or other decorations.

■ Yarn Doll
[Makes 1]

Yarn dolls are soft and cuddly. They could be made much larger than the instructions indicate.

Materials

about 10 yards yarn   scissors
cardboard scrap about 8 inches wide

Procedure

1. Wind the yarn around the cardboard at least 16 times and cut at the end of the last wind.
2. Cut 7 pieces of yarn about 10 inches each.
3. Cut the yarn wound around the cardboard and remove the cardboard.
4. Fold the yarn strands you have just cut in half so the ends are even. Tie one 10-inch piece of yarn around the yarn strands about 1 inch down from the uncut end to form the head.
5. Pull away 8 strands of yarn from the body to form an arm. Tie with a 10-inch piece of yarn to form a shoulder. Cut off some of the yarn so that the arm is not too long. Tie the arm at the wrist with a 10-inch piece of the yarn.
6. Repeat for the other arm.
7. With another 10-inch piece of yarn, tie the remaining 16 pieces to form a waist.
8. For a girl doll, trim the yarn to form the bottom of the skirt.
9. For a boy doll, pull away 8 strands and tie at the ankle with one 10-inch piece of yarn.
10. Repeat for the other leg.

■ Cup and Ball Toy
[Makes 1]

This toy was originally made from wood. The wooden ball stung when it hit a child. Making the cup and ball is easy. Getting the ball into the cup takes coordination and patience. The ball is made out of aluminum foil so that it does not hurt the player.

Materials

1 tongue depressor
1 paper cup
1 piece of string about 18 inches long
1 piece of aluminum foil about
    12 inches by 12 inches

scissors
hot glue gun and hot glue

Procedure

1. Make a small slit in the bottom of the paper cup with the scissors.

2. Insert the tongue depressor about 1 inch into the slit and hot glue the paper cup and tongue depressor together.

3. Tie one end of the string around the tongue depressor where it meets the cup.

4. Crush the aluminum foil around the other end of the string and make a small ball. You may want to first tie a knot at the end of the string.

5. Try to swing the ball and catch it in the cup.

■ Humming Whirligig Toy
[Makes 1]

I can make these, but I cannot make them hum. Other people take my whirligigs and make them hum nicely. I cannot skip rocks either.

Materials

flat button with at least 2 holes
string that is thin enough to pass
    through buttonholes.

scissors

Procedure

1. String the thread through the buttonholes and tie the ends. This will make a loop. The loop should be a bit longer than your body is wide.

2. Stretch the loop to its full length. Make sure the button is in the middle of the loop. Twist the string in one direction until it is wound tightly.

3. Pull your arms apart and then together again. Repeat the process.

4. Soon your button will be twirling and humming.

■ Braided Rug (or Hot Pad)

[Makes 1]

Braided rugs were a good way to cover the floor. Scraps of leftover fabric or fabric from discarded clothing were used to make brightly colored rugs.

Materials

3 strips of fabric at least 2 yards long
  and about 1 inch wide

2 safety pins
needle and thread

Procedure

1. Pin together the ends of the 3 pieces of fabric with one safety pin.
2. Have another child hold the ends, or tie string to the safety pin and tie the string around something sturdy like a table leg.
3. Begin to braid the 3 strips as tightly as possible.
4. When the fabric has been completely braided, fasten the ends with the other safety pin.
5. Sew the ends together with the needle and thread.
6. Tightly curl the braid so that it forms a compact spiral. Stitch the spiral together every inch or so along the way.

■ Quill Pen

[Makes 1]

Writing with a quill pen is difficult. Ink sometimes goes where it should not go. Colonial children spent about half their school day working on penmanship. Now I see why.

Materials

goose quill or any other feather at least 11 inches long (can be obtained from craft stores or poultry farms)

warm, soapy water in a small container

scissors

pin

piece of felt about 6 inches by 6 inches

ink

paper

Procedure

1. Soak the bottom of the quill in the warm, soapy water for about 20 minutes.
2. Remove the feathers from the bottom 2 inches of the quill.
3. Cut off the bottom of the quill at an angle. This will become the nib of the pen.
4. Clean out the inside of the nib with the pin.
5. Cut a lengthwise slit about half an inch long beginning at the point of the nib.
6. Dip the nib into the ink and carefully blot onto the felt. This will remove excess ink.
7. To write, hold the pen at a slant. This will take practice.
8. When the nib is worn down, repeat the steps to create a new one.

■ Soot Ink

[Makes about ¼ cup]

This ink is a simplified version of a very old recipe. This ink will not keep well unless it is refrigerated. Inks used long ago spoiled quickly and were therefore made in small batches.

Materials

about 3 tablespoons soot collected from sides of fireplaces

1 egg white

about 2 tablespoons honey

whisk

disposable container

disposable spoon

small jar with lid

Procedure

1. Pour the egg white into the disposable container. Beat the egg white with the whisk for just a few seconds.
2. Add the soot and mix well.
3. Add enough honey to make a creamy consistency.
4. Pour into small jar and put the lid on.

■ Berry Ink
[Makes about ½ cup]

This ink spoils quickly. It should be refrigerated.

Materials

1 cup ripe berries
small piece of cheesecloth
small bowl
1 teaspoon salt

1 teaspoon vinegar
spoon
small jar with lid

Procedure

1. Line the small bowl with the cheesecloth.
2. Pour the berries into the cheesecloth.
3. Pick up the cheesecloth to make a small bag and squeeze the berries so that the juice trickles into the small bowl.
4. Add the vinegar and salt, and stir until the salt dissolves.
5. Pour the berry ink into the small jar and put the lid on.

■ Walnut Shell Ink
[Makes about 1 cup]

The salt and vinegar stabilize the color and keep the ink from spoiling too fast.

Materials

20 walnut shells
plastic bag
hammer
2 cups water
1½ teaspoons vinegar
1½ teaspoons salt

old pot
heating element
spoon
small piece of cheesecloth
jar with lid

Procedure

1. Pour the walnut shells into the plastic bag.
2. Crush the shells with the hammer.
3. Pour the crushed shells into the old pot and add the water.
4. Heat the mixture until it boils and then let simmer for about an hour. The water should be dark brown. Allow to cool.
5. Strain the mixture through the cheesecloth into the jar.
6. Add the vinegar and salt, and stir.
7. Put the lid on the jar.

■ Signet
[Makes 1]

Signets were used to seal envelopes. A signet acted somewhat like a signature. Since a signet is pressed into warm wax, its impression is the opposite of what is designed.

Materials

rectangular piece of self-hardening clay about 3 inches by 1 inch by 1 inch
pencil

tweezers
vegetable oil
cotton swab
sealing wax (see next recipe)

Procedure

1. Stand the clay on one end so that the top is 1 inch by 1 inch.
2. Use the pencil to lightly draw the signet design. If a letter is used, make sure the letter is drawn backwards.
3. Use the tweezers to dig the clay away from the design so that the design stands in relief. Let the clay harden overnight.
4. Use the swab to apply a small amount of vegetable oil to the signet before stamping it into the warm wax. The oil will keep the wax from sticking to the signet.

■ Sealing Wax
[Makes 1 sealed letter]

Self-sealing envelopes are rather new. Years ago people made envelopes from the letter itself by folding it and sealing it with wax. Sealing wax was available in only two colors, red and black. Black sealing wax was used only when a family was mourning the death of a loved one. Red sealing wax was used for all other occasions.

Materials

hand-written letter
old candle, preferably red
match

signet (see activity above) or other 3-dimensional object to press into hot wax, such as a coin or the tines of a fork

Procedure

1. Fold the corners of the letter so that they meet in the middle. The writing should be inside the folds.
2. Light the old candle with the match. Wait a minute or so and drip some of the hot wax onto where the folds meet in the middle.
3. Quickly press the 3-dimensional object into the hot wax and remove. An impression of the object should remain.
4. Let the wax cool.

■ Tin Punching
[Makes 1 project]

Tin punching was quite an art, and it still is. Tin lanterns were punched so that the light could show through the holes. Tin plates were punched and used as decorations. This procedure requires that water be frozen in the container to make it easier to punch. Students should wear safety goggles and gloves because pieces of ice could fly about.

Materials

1 smooth can or paint container
old towel
1 piece of paper with pattern of dots
tape
water

hammer and nail
votive candle
match
safety goggles
gloves

Procedure

1. Fill the container with water and place it in the freezer for at least a day.

2. Remove the container from the freezer and place it on its side on the towel. The towel will keep it in place.

3. Students should wear safety goggles and gloves.

4. Tape the paper pattern to the side of the container.

5. Use the hammer to punch the nail through the paper pattern and side of the container at every dot. Watch out for pieces of loose ice.

6. When the pattern has been completely punched out, remove the paper pattern and turn the container over. Allow the ice to melt enough to empty the container.

7. After the container is dry, set the votive candle on the bottom of the inside of the container.

8. Light the candle. The light should shine through the holes.

CHAPTER
21
Candy

Students love to make candy. Here are plenty of easy-to-use recipes. Many of these recipes require little time because they use a microwave oven instead of a stove. Only one recipe needs a candy thermometer.

■ Irish Potato Candy
[Makes about 25]

These candies are popular around St. Patrick's Day. Potatoes are an important part of Ireland's heritage, and these candies make St. Patrick's Day special.

Materials

One 8-ounce package of cream cheese	cinnamon
2 cups sifted confectioners' sugar	mixing bowl
1 ounce shredded coconut	spoon
1 teaspoon vanilla	wax paper

Procedure

1. Combine the first four ingredients in the mixing bowl.
2. Spread the cinnamon on the wax paper.
3. Divide the mixture into portions about the size of a large marble.
4. Roll each portion into a ball and then roll the portions in the cinnamon.
5. Keep refrigerated.

■ Irish Mashed Potato Candy

[Makes 36 pieces]

These candies are also popular around St. Patrick's Day. This recipe uses actual potatoes.

Materials

½ cup mashed potatoes (cooked with
    no added ingredients)
1 teaspoon vanilla
1 pound confectioners' sugar
2 tablespoons cinnamon
mixing bowl

mixing spoon
wax paper
tray or cookie sheet
small plastic bag
airtight container

Procedure

1. Combine the mashed potatoes and vanilla in the mixing bowl.

2. Gradually add the confectioners' sugar, stirring constantly. The dough should become stiff but not sticky.

3. Remove about 1 teaspoonful of dough at a time. Form "potatoes" and set on the wax paper-lined tray to dry slightly.

4. Pour the cinnamon into the plastic bag. Place several potatoes in the bag and toss gently.

5. Remove and shake off excess cinnamon.

6. Store in an airtight container.

■ Very Easy Fudge

[Makes 24 pieces]

Fudge actually uses some of the science of crystallization. This particular recipe requires little cooking.

Materials

2 packages semi-sweet chocolate
    (8 squares each)
one 14-ounce can sweetened
    condensed milk
2 teaspoons vanilla
small amount of shortening

1 microwave-safe mixing bowl
microwave oven
one 8 inch by 8 inch square pan
spoon
can opener

Procedure

1. Combine chocolate and milk in microwave-safe mixing bowl.
2. Microwave mixture for 1 minute.
3. Stir and microwave for about 1 or 2 minutes.
4. Stir until chocolate is melted.
5. Add the vanilla and stir again.
6. Grease the square pan with the shortening.
7. Pour into greased pan and refrigerate until firm.
8. Cut into pieces.

■ Caramel Apples

[Makes 4 apples]

Watch out for the caramel—make sure it is not too hot.

Materials

4 medium apples
4 wooden sticks
one 14-ounce bag of caramels,
    unwrapped
small amount of shortening

2 tablespoons water
large microwave-safe mixing bowl
microwave oven
spoon
wax paper

Procedure

1. Combine unwrapped caramels and water in microwave-safe mixing bowl.
2. Microwave on high for several minutes, until the caramels are melted.
3. Place a wooden stick into the stem end of each apple.
4. Dip each apple into the caramel mixture and coat.
5. Grease the wax paper with the shortening.
6. Place each apple on the greased wax paper and cool.
7. Do not refrigerate.

■ Popcorn Balls

[Makes 12 balls, each 3 inches in diameter]

The sugar mixture can be very hot, so students should be very careful.

Materials

½ cup sugar
½ cup brown sugar
½ cup light corn syrup
⅓ cup water
1 cup (2 sticks) butter, cut into pieces
4 cups popped popcorn
enough butter to butter hands

pot
heating element
candy thermometer
large mixing bowl, lightly oiled
spoon
wax paper
plastic wrap

Procedure

1. Combine sugars and corn syrup in pot and bring to a boil.
2. Add butter and stir. Cook for 20 to 30 minutes until the mixture reads 300° F on candy thermometer.
3. Pour popcorn into large mixing bowl.
4. Drizzle mixture over the popcorn and mix.
5. Butter hands so that the popcorn will not stick to skin.
6. As soon as the mixture cools, quickly shape into 3-inch balls.
7. Place balls on wax paper until they cool.
8. Wrap balls individually in plastic wrap to keep them fresh.

■ Jelly Bean Nests
[Makes 12 nests]

These treats are great to make around Easter.

Materials

2 cups miniature marshmallows
¼ cup (½ stick) butter
4 cups chow mein noodles
extra butter
jelly beans

microwave-safe mixing bowl
microwave oven
spoon
12-cup muffin pan

Procedure

1. Combine marshmallows and butter in microwave-safe mixing bowl.
2. Microwave on high for about 3 minutes, stirring every minute or so, until the marshmallows are melted.
3. Stir in chow mein noodles.
4. Butter the muffin cups.
5. With buttered fingers, press some of the mixture into each of the muffin cups.
6. Refrigerate for several hours.
7. Remove nests from muffin cups and add jelly beans.

■ Chocolate Marshmallow Spiders
[Makes 24 cookies]

These treats are great to make at Halloween.

Materials

8 squares semisweet baking
    chocolate
2 cups miniature marshmallows
string licorice
various candies

microwave-safe bowl
microwave oven
mixing spoon
wax paper
tray

Procedure

1. Place the baking chocolate in the microwave-safe bowl and microwave until melted (about 2 minutes).
2. Stir until completely melted.
3. Add marshmallows and stir until combined with the chocolate.
4. Line the tray with wax paper.
5. Drop the mixture by spoonfuls onto the wax paper.
6. Add the licorice strings to form legs.
7. Use candies to create eyes and other details.
8. Refrigerate until firm.

■ Marshmallow Ghosts

[Makes about 30 ghosts]

These goodies are also fun to make at Halloween.

Materials

4 packages (6 ounces each) white chocolate baking squares	microwave oven
3 cups miniature marshmallows	mixing spoon
various candies or icing	wax paper
microwave-safe bowl	trays

Procedure

1. Microwave the white chocolate baking squares in the microwave-safe bowl until melted (about 3 to 4 minutes).

2. Stir to make the mixture smooth. Let cool for a few minutes.

3. Add the marshmallows and combine.

4. Place the wax paper on the trays.

5. Drop the mixture by spoonfuls on the wax paper.

6. Decorate with candies and icing.

■ Chocolate-Covered Pretzel Rods

[Makes 10]

Students could dunk other foods in the melted chocolate. Dried fruits, fresh strawberries, and chunks of bananas are good candidates.

Materials

1 cup chocolate chips	microwave oven
ten 8-inch pretzel rods	mixing spoon
colored sprinkles in a small bowl	wax paper
microwave-safe bowl	

Procedure

1. Pour the chocolate chips into the microwave-safe bowl and microwave until melted (about 1 to 2 minutes).

2. Stir to make mixture smooth.

3. Dunk the pretzel rods into the chocolate and then into the bowl of sprinkles.

4. Place on wax paper until chocolate hardens.

■ Chocolate Peanut Butter Pizza
[Makes 16 small slices]

Students can learn about fractions as they cut their chocolate peanut butter pizzas. Make sure no student is allergic to nuts.

Materials

one 6-ounce package chocolate chips
one 6-ounce package peanut butter
    chips
2 ounces white baking chocolate
various candies
2 microwave-safe bowls

microwave oven
mixing spoon
12-inch pizza pan
enough grease to coat pizza pan
spatula
pizza wheel or knife

Procedure

1. Microwave the chocolate chips and the peanut butter chips in one microwave-safe bowl until melted (about 2 minutes).
2. Stir to blend the chips.
3. Grease the pizza pan.
4. Spread the melted mixture onto the pizza pan with the spatula.
5. Microwave the white baking chocolate in the other microwave-safe bowl until it is melted (about 1 minute).
6. Drizzle mixture over the melted chip mixture so that it looks like cheese.
7. Decorate with various candies.
8. Refrigerate for about a half hour.
9. Cut into 16 wedges and serve.

■ Peanut Butter Turtles

[Makes 10 to 12]

Make sure no one is allergic to nuts because this recipe uses peanut butter. Students could learn about real turtles as they munch their peanut butter turtles.

Materials

½ cup peanut butter
3 ounces cream cheese, softened
2 tablespoons honey
1 cup granola or crunchy cereal
slivered almonds

raisins
mixing bowl
mixing spoon
wax paper
tray or cookie sheet

Procedure

1. Combine the peanut butter, cream cheese, and honey in the mixing bowl.
2. Gently mix in the cereal.
3. Place wax paper on the tray.
4. Drop the mixture by spoonfuls on the tray.
5. Shape each mixture to look like the body of a turtle.
6. Place the slivered almonds to look like legs and the raisins to look like eyes.
7. Refrigerate until firm.

■ Frosting-Pudding Candy

[Makes about 30 pieces]

Pistachio pudding would make a good flavor of this candy.

Materials

1 can prepared vanilla frosting
1 small box pudding mix
coconut
2 mixing bowls

mixing spoon
wax paper
tray

Procedure

1. Combine the frosting and pudding in one mixing bowl.
2. Place coconut in the other mixing bowl.
3. Form the candy into balls and roll in coconut.
4. Line tray with wax paper.
5. Place candy on tray and refrigerate until candy is firm (about 2 hours).

■ Mints
[Makes about 30 pieces]

These mints could change with the holidays. Red food coloring could be used for St. Valentine's Day. Pastel colors could be used at Easter. Orange mints could be made for Halloween. Red and green colors could make Christmas mints.

Materials

3 tablespoons butter
3 tablespoons milk
1 box white frosting mix
food coloring
½ teaspoon peppermint extract

microwave-safe bowl
microwave oven
mixing spoon
wax paper
airtight container

Procedure

1. Combine the milk and butter in the microwave-safe bowl.

2. Microwave the mixture for about a minute or until the butter melts.

3. Add the frosting mix.

4. Microwave on high for about 2 minutes until the mixture bubbles. Stir once about halfway through the cooking.

5. Remove from the microwave and add the food coloring and peppermint extract.

6. Drop small amounts onto the wax paper to cool.

7. Store in an airtight container.

■ Peanut Butter Fudge
[Makes about 20 pieces]

This fudge tastes good, but it remains somewhat soft when it is at room temperature. Make sure no student is allergic to nuts.

Materials

one 18-ounce jar of peanut butter
1 can of ready-made vanilla frosting
mixing bowl

mixing spoon
One 9 inch by 9 inch pan
airtight container

Procedure

1. Combine the peanut butter and frosting in the mixing bowl.

2. Pour the mixture into the pan.

3. Refrigerate.

4. Store in an airtight container.

■ Natural Fruit Candy
[Makes 1 pound, about 20 pieces]

Use only one type of dried fruit. Otherwise, the colors may not be so pretty. Make sure no student is allergic to nuts.

Materials

1 pound dried fruit
about ½ cup fruit juice
½ cup finely chopped nuts
food processor

spoon
small bowl
wax paper
cookie sheet

Procedure

1. Pour the dried fruit into the food processor and grind.
2. Add enough fruit juice to make the ground fruit stick together.
3. Pour the chopped nuts into the small bowl.
4. Line the cookie sheet with wax paper.
5. Remove the top of the food processor and spoon out small amounts of the fruit candy. Form small balls.
6. Coat the small fruit balls in the nuts and place on the wax paper.
7. Store in an airtight container.

22
Fruit Preserves

Fruit preserves were first made to take advantage of summer's bountiful fruit. The fruit preserves were stored away until they could be used in winter. Jams, jellies, fruit butters, and marmalades are the most common types of fruit preserves. Most fruit preserves are canned, but that takes time. Also, it is not always safe because processing requires water baths with high temperatures. Furthermore, microbes can still enter the preserves. These freezer and refrigerator recipes require no processing and they taste good. The high sugar content actually keeps microbes away. Fruit should be at room temperature when any preserve is made. Pectin can be purchased in the canning section of the grocery store.

■ Raspberry-Blueberry Refrigerator Jam
[Makes 1 cup]

Raspberries and blueberries are expensive, but they provide a great treat. Consider buying these and freezing them in the summertime when prices are more reasonable.

Materials

¾ cup blueberries
¾ cup raspberries
2½ teaspoons powdered pectin
½ cup sugar

2-quart microwave-safe bowl
microwave oven
mixing spoon
storage container and lid

Procedure

1. Combine the blueberries, raspberries, and pectin in the microwave-safe bowl.

2. Microwave for about 2 minutes until the mixture is bubbling.

3. Add the sugar and microwave for 3 more minutes.

4. Skim off the foam and pour into the storage container.

5. Allow to cool. Add the lid and refrigerate.

6. Use within 2 weeks.

■ Strawberry Freezer Jam

[Makes 4¾ cups]

Make sure the strawberries are firm and unbruised.

Materials

1 quart strawberries, washed and
    hulled
4 cups sugar
¾ cup water
⅓ cup pectin
mixing bowl

potato masher
pot
heating element
mixing spoon
clean freezer containers with lids

Procedure

1. In the mixing bowl lightly crush the strawberries with the potato masher and add the sugar. Let this mixture sit for 10 minutes.
2. In the pot combine the water and pectin. Bring to a boil and cook, stirring constantly, for 1 minute.
3. Remove the pot from the heat. Pour the pectin-water mixture into the fruit mixture and stir for 3 minutes.
4. Pour the mixture into freezer containers and quickly cover with lids. Keep at room temperature for a day and then freeze.
5. After removing from freezer, keep in refrigerator. Use within 2 weeks.

■ Grape Freezer Jelly

[Makes 6⅓ cups]

You could make your own juice, but the bottled variety works almost as well.

Materials

3 cups unsweetened grape juice
5¼ cups sugar
¾ cup water
⅓ cup pectin
mixing bowl

pot
heating element
mixing spoon
clean freezer containers with lids

Procedure

1. In the mixing bowl combine the juice and sugar. Let this mixture sit for 10 minutes.
2. In the pot combine the water and pectin. Bring to a boil and cook, stirring constantly, for 1 minute.
3. Stir the pectin-water mixture into the juice mixture and stir for 3 minutes.
4. Pour mixture into freezer containers and quickly cover with lids. Keep at room temperature for a day and then freeze.
5. After removing from freezer, keep in refrigerator. Use within 2 weeks.

■ Peach Freezer Jam
[Makes 5⅔ cups]

The lemon juice and the ascorbic acid preservative keep the peaches from turning brown.

Materials

2¼ cups peaches, peeled, pitted and chopped (about 2 pounds)
2 tablespoons lemon juice
1 teaspoon ascorbic acid preservative
5 cups sugar
¾ cup water

⅓ cup pectin
mixing bowl
pot
heating element
mixing spoon
clean freezer containers with lids

Procedure

1. In the mixing bowl combine the peaches, lemon juice, ascorbic acid preservative, and sugar.

2. In the pot combine the water and pectin. Bring to a boil and cook, stirring constantly, for 1 minute.

3. Remove the pot from the heat. Stir the pectin-water mixture into the fruit mixture and stir for 3 minutes.

4. Pour mixture into freezer containers and quickly cover with lids. Keep at room temperature for a day and then freeze.

5. After removing from freezer, keep in refrigerator. Use within 2 weeks.

■ Rhubarb-Cherry Freezer Jam

[Makes 2 pints]

When we eat rhubarb, we are eating the stem of the plant. Rhubarb leaves contain poisonous substances. Rhubarb by itself is quite tart. This recipe requires 2 days.

Materials

6 cups peeled, sliced rhubarb
4 cups sugar
1 can (21 ounces) cherry pie filling
1 package (6 ounces) cherry-flavored gelatin
mixing bowl and cover

mixing spoon
pot
heating element
shallow container
clean freezer containers with lids

Procedure

1. Combine the rhubarb and sugar in the mixing bowl. Cover and refrigerate overnight.
2. Pour the rhubarb-sugar mixture into the pot and cook over medium heat until the rhubarb is tender.
3. Remove from heat and add the cherry pie filling and gelatin.
4. Pour into the shallow container and refrigerate.
5. When the mixture is cold, place in freezer containers. Cover with lids and place in freezer.
6. After removing from freezer, keep in refrigerator. Use within 2 weeks.

■ Pumpkin Butter

[Makes 2 cups]

Similar to apple butter, this fruit spread is delicious on waffles and muffins.

Materials

1 can (15 ounces) pumpkin puree
1 cup applesauce
⅓ cup packed brown sugar
1 teaspoon cinnamon
1 teaspoon ground ginger

2½ tablespoons lemon juice
pot
heating element
mixing spoon
clean container with lid

Procedure

1. Combine all the ingredients except the lemon juice in the pot.
2. Heat until the mixture begins to boil, and then reduce the temperature to a simmer. Cook, stirring often, for about an hour or until the pumpkin butter is very thick.
3. Add the lemon juice and stir well.
4. Allow the mixture to cool and then pour into the clean container. Add the lid and refrigerate.
5. Use within 2 weeks.

■ Orange-Pineapple Marmalade
[Makes 4 cups]

A marmalade uses the fruit peel as well as the fruit. This recipe uses a microwave and not a stove. Make sure that the microwave-safe container is deep, because the sauce expands as it cooks in the microwave.

Materials

2 large oranges	knife
1 can (15½ ounces) crushed pineapple with the juice removed	microwave-safe container microwave oven
4 cups sugar	mixing spoon
2½ tablespoons lemon juice	clean freezer containers with lids

Procedure

1. Wash and cut the oranges. Remove the seeds.

2. Cut the orange pieces into very fine pieces.

3. Combine the oranges with the other ingredients in the microwave-safe container and microwave at high, stirring occasionally, for about 8 minutes until the mixture begins to boil.

4. Microwave at high for another 2 to 3 minutes.

5. Pour the marmalade into the clean freezer containers with lids.

6. Cool for 4 hours at room temperature, then freeze.

7. The marmalade can remain in the freezer for a year, or it can stay in the refrigerator for about 2 weeks.

23
Syrups

Real maple syrup is made from the sap of maple trees. The sap is collected in the early spring. About 25 gallons of sap are boiled down to make 1 gallon of maple syrup. Making real maple syrup in a classroom is not possible, but fruit syrups are easy to make. These syrups go well with waffles, pancakes, and French toast. They could also act as toppings for ice cream and yogurt desserts.

■ Blueberry Syrup

[Makes 1 cup]

Nutritionists say blueberries are extremely nutritious. They are low in calories, and they contain high amounts of antioxidants.

Materials

2 cups fresh or frozen blueberries
½ cup water
½ cup sugar
2 teaspoons lemon juice

pot
heating element
mixing spoon

Procedure

1. In the pot combine 1 cup blueberries, water, sugar, and lemon juice.
2. Cook over medium heat, stirring constantly, until the sugar dissolves.
3. Bring to a boil and then reduce heat to simmer. Cook, stirring constantly, for about 20 minutes until mixture is thick.
4. Add remaining blueberries and simmer for about 3 more minutes.
5. Remove pot from the heating element and allow syrup to cool.
6. Syrup can be stored in the refrigerator for about a week.

■ Grape Syrup

[Makes 1¾ cups]

This recipe is probably the easiest and cheapest to make.

Materials

1 cup grape jam or jelly
½ cup light corn syrup
¼ cup water

pot
heating element
mixing spoon

Procedure

1. In the pot combine the grape jam or jelly, corn syrup, and water. Stir over medium heat until the jelly melts.
2. Serve warm.
3. Syrup can be stored in the refrigerator for about a week.

■ Cranberry Syrup

[Makes 2 cups]

Cranberries by themselves are quite tart.

Materials

2½ cups cranberry juice
¾ cup light corn syrup
½ cup sugar

pot
heating element
mixing spoon

Procedure

1. In the pot combine the cranberry juice, corn syrup, and sugar. Stir over medium heat until the sugar dissolves.
2. Bring to a boil and let simmer for about a half hour.
3. Serve warm.
4. Syrup can be stored in the refrigerator for about a week.

■ Peanut Butter Syrup

[Makes 1½ cups]

Peanut butter syrup should not be eaten by anyone who is allergic to nuts.

Materials

4 tablespoons butter or margarine
⅓ cup creamy peanut butter
1 cup maple-flavored syrup
½ cup water

pot
heating element
mixing spoon

Procedure

1. Melt the butter in the pot over low heat.
2. Stir in the peanut butter.
3. Add the syrup and water and combine.
4. Bring to a boil, stirring constantly.
5. Simmer for about 5 minutes or until slightly thickened.
6. Serve warm.
7. Syrup can be stored in the refrigerator for about a week.

■ Brown Sugar Syrup
[Makes 1⅔ cups]

This syrup is particularly good over ice cream.

Materials

2 cups packed brown sugar
1 cup water
1½ teaspoons vanilla

pot
heating element
mixing spoon

Procedure

1. Combine the brown sugar and water in the pot. Stir over medium heat until brown sugar melts.
2. Bring to a boil and reduce heat. Cook, stirring constantly, on low heat for about 5 minutes.
3. Remove from heat and add vanilla.
4. Serve warm.
5. Syrup can be stored in the refrigerator for about a week.

■ Apple-Maple Syrup
[Makes 1 cup]

Students could find out how apple cider differs from apple juice.

Materials

1 cup apple cider
1 cup maple-flavored syrup
pot

heating element
mixing spoon

Procedure

1. Combine the cider and syrup in the pot.
2. Bring to a boil and reduce heat. Cook, stirring constantly, on low heat for about 15 minutes until syrup is thick.
3. Serve warm.
4. Syrup can be stored in the refrigerator for about a week.

■ Orange Syrup
[Makes 1 cup]

Students could find out how maple syrup is different from maple-flavored syrup. There are several grades of real maple syrup. How does one grade differ from another?

Materials

1 cup maple-flavored syrup   heating element
1 orange, sliced   mixing spoon
pot

Procedure

1. Combine the syrup and orange slices in the pot.
2. Bring to a boil and reduce heat. Cook, stirring constantly, on low heat for about 5 minutes.
3. Remove from heat, and remove orange slices.
4. Serve warm.
5. Syrup can be stored in the refrigerator for about a week.

24

Pickles, Sauerkraut, Mustards, and Horseradish

Pickling, a method of preserving food, dates back to very early cultures. The high salt and vinegar content discourages the growth of microbes. Today the ability to refrigerate and freeze fruits and vegetables has made pickling less necessary. True pickling requires canning, which takes a great deal of time and preparation. It can also be dangerous, because high temperatures are necessary to kill bacteria. The following recipes do not require canning, but they do give students a sense of how to preserve foods.

■ Refrigerator Pickles
[Makes 6 cups]

The vinegar and salt form the brine, which preserves vegetables. The solution is so acidic that bacteria cannot grow in it.

Materials

6 cups thinly sliced cucumbers	1½ cups vinegar
1½ cups sugar	large, very clean jar
½ teaspoon salt	pot
½ teaspoon mustard seed	heating element
½ teaspoon celery seed	mixing spoon
½ teaspoon turmeric	

Procedure

1. Layer the cucumbers and onions in the large jar.
2. Combine the other ingredients in the pot.
3. Bring the mixture to a boil, stirring until the sugar is dissolved.
4. Remove the mixture from the heat and pour over the cucumbers and onions.
5. Cool for about 2 hours and then cover tightly and refrigerate for several days.
6. Eat the pickles within about 2 weeks.

■ Refrigerator Dill Pickles
[Makes about 9 cups]

Dill is an herb that students could easily grow indoors and then transplant in the springtime.

Materials

10 cucumbers	knife
1 cup vinegar	pot
1 cup water	heating element
1 tablespoon salt	mixing spoon
2 tablespoons dill	large crock or glass bowl with lid or
1 clove garlic, crushed	plastic wrap
½ teaspoon mustard seeds	

Procedure

1. Wash cucumbers and slice with the knife.
2. Combine the water, vinegar, and salt in the pot and bring to a boil. This will form a brine.
3. Place a layer of dill, crushed garlic, and mustard seeds in the bottom of the crock.
4. Place cucumbers on top of the herbs.
5. Add another layer of dill.
6. Cover the cucumbers with the brine mixture.
7. Cover and place in the refrigerator for several days.
8. Eat the pickles within about 2 weeks.

■ Refrigerator Bread-and-Butter Pickles

[Makes 1 quart]

The sugar and the vinegar give these pickles a sweet-and-sour taste.

Materials

1 quart cucumbers	1¼ teaspoon salt
1 sliced onion	large pot
1 cup sugar	heating element
1 teaspoon turmeric	mixing spoon
½ teaspoon mustard seeds	large crock or glass bowl with lid or
1 cup vinegar	plastic wrap

Procedure

1. Wash and slice the cucumbers.

2. In the large pot combine the sugar, turmeric, mustard seeds, vinegar, and salt. Bring to a boil.

3. Add the cucumbers and sliced onions and bring the mixture to a boil again.

4. Remove the pot from the heating element and allow the mixture to cool for about a half hour.

5. Pour the mixture into the crock and cover. Refrigerate for several days.

6. Eat the pickles within about 2 weeks.

■ Sauerkraut

[Makes about 1 gallon]

Sauerkraut is a way of preserving cabbage. The salt creates an environment that keeps bacteria away. Note that the volume of cabbage greatly reduces when it becomes sauerkraut.

Materials

about 5 pounds of cabbage
knife
3½ tablespoons salt
large crock or jar
wooden spoon

clean cloth
plate big enough to cover mouth of crock or jar
a weight to keep plate on top of crock or jar

Procedure

1. Shred the cabbage.
2. Layer the cabbage and salt in the crock or jar.
3. Cover with the cloth, plate, and weight.
4. Each day for about 10 days, skim the scum from the top of the mixture.
5. Thoroughly rinse the cloth daily to prevent mold.
6. In about 10 days fermentation should be complete, and the sauerkraut can be tasted.
7. Refrigerate and consume within several days.

■ All-Purpose Mustard

[Makes ⅔ cup]

Homemade (or school-made) mustard is likely to be more watery and stronger flavored than commercial mustards. Any mustard should mellow for at least a full day before being tasted.

Materials

2 tablespoons coarsely ground brown mustard seeds
2 tablespoons coarsely ground yellow mustard seeds
¼ cup mustard powder
¼ cup cold water

2 tablespoons vinegar
½ teaspoon salt
mixing bowl
mixing spoon
jar with lid

Procedure

1. Combine the ground brown and yellow mustard seeds, mustard powder, and water in the mixing bowl. Let stand for 10 minutes.
2. Stir in vinegar and salt.
3. Pour into jar and screw on the lid. Refrigerate for at least 24 hours before serving.
4. Consume the mustard within about 2 weeks.

■ Sweet-Hot Mustard
[Makes about 1½ cups]

Different types of mustard are available. Some are stronger than others. Students could grind mustard seeds and try out different types.

Materials

4 ounces dry mustard powder	double boiler
3 eggs	water for double boiler
1 cup apple cider vinegar	heating element
1 cup brown sugar	mixing spoon
blender	jar and lid

Procedure

1. Combine all the ingredients in the blender and blend until smooth.
2. Pour the mixture into the top of a double boiler. Place water in the bottom of the double boiler.
3. Bring almost to a boil and then reduce heat. Cook until thickened.
4. Pour the mixture into the jar and let cool. Screw on the lid.
5. Refrigerate and let mellow for at least 24 hours.
6. Consume the mustard within about 2 weeks.

■ Honey Mustard
[Makes about 1¼ cups]

The honey gives this mustard a bit of sweetness.

Materials

⅓ cup dry mustard	1 teaspoon Worcestershire sauce
½ cup honey	mixing bowl
½ cup brown sugar	mixing spoon
¼ cup vinegar	jar and lid
¼ cup vegetable oil	

Procedure

1. Combine all the ingredients in the mixing bowl.
2. Pour into the jar and refrigerate for at least 24 hours.
3. Consume the mustard within about 2 weeks.

■ Horseradish

[Makes about 1 cup]

Horseradish has been consumed for thousands of years. Horseradish is one of the bitter herbs served at Passover meals. The Greeks used ground horseradish as a salve for back pain. American colonists grew it in their gardens and used it to flavor stews and many types of meats.

Materials

1 large, fresh horseradish root
    (no soft spots or green coloring)
vegetable peeler
knife

grater
wax paper
vinegar or sour cream (optional)
clean jar with lid

Procedure

1. Peel off the outer layer of the horseradish root.

2. Cut the root into slices and remove the fibrous core.

3. Grate the root over a piece of wax paper.

4. Serve as is or mix with vinegar or sour cream.

5. Store in a jar with the lid screwed on tightly.

6. Refrigerate. Consume the horseradish within about 2 weeks.

25
Treats That Students Can Make

The following recipes fall into several categories. Some, like hot cocoa and doughnuts, are just nice treats. I chose to include several types of flat bread, including pita, chappatis, and crepes, because almost every culture has some sort of flat bread. Finally, I added some recipes, like pemmican, that make learning about a culture fun and interesting.

■ Hot Cocoa for a Crowd

[Makes 16 to 20 servings]

Water could be heated ahead of time in a Crock Pot; the hot cocoa could follow a cold, windy, winter recess.

Materials

2 cups powdered milk	large mixing bowl
⅓ cup cocoa	mixing spoon
1 cup confectioners' sugar	hot cups
⅓ cup powdered nondairy creamer	boiling water
½ teaspoon salt	ladle

Procedure

1. Combine the powdered milk, cocoa, confectioners' sugar, nondairy creamer, and salt in the bowl.

2. Each cup of cocoa needs about four tablespoons of the mix and boiling water.

■ Lemonade for a Crowd

[Makes 20 servings]

This cool treat could follow field day activities.

Materials

4 quarts water	large mixing spoon
3 cups lemon juice	ladle
4 cups sugar	paper or plastic cups
large pot or container	ice

Procedure

1. Combine the water and lemon juice in the large container.

2. Stir in the sugar.

3. Place ice in cups and then add lemonade.

■ Marshmallows

[Makes about 20]

The gelatin forms a colloid, and air is trapped within the colloid to produce puffy marshmallows.

Materials

2 tablespoons (2 packets) unflavored
    gelatin
1 cup boiling water
1 cup sugar
2½ teaspoons vanilla
confectioners' sugar
mixing bowl

mixing spoon
egg beater
wax paper
shortening to grease the wax paper
shallow pan
knife

Procedure

1. Combine the unflavored gelatin and boiling water in the mixing bowl.

2. Gradually add the sugar and vanilla.

3. Beat with the eggbeater until the mixture becomes marshmallow cream. This may take about 15 to 20 minutes.

4. Grease the wax paper and place in a shallow pan.

5. Pour the marshmallow cream onto the wax paper.

6. Cover loosely with more wax paper. Make sure the top wax paper does not touch the marshmallow cream.

7. Let the pan sit overnight. The next day cut the hardened marshmallow mixture into cubes and dust with confectioners' sugar.

■ Matzo

[Makes 8 to 10 matzos, enough to serve a class of about 30 students]

Matzo is eaten during Passover. Jews do not eat leavened bread during Passover.

Materials

2 cups matzo meal
about 1½ cups water
¾ teaspoon salt
mixing bowl
mixing spoon
working surface with extra matzo meal

wax paper
rolling pin
fork
cookie sheets
oven
spatula

Procedure

1. Combine in the mixing bowl the matzo meal, salt, and enough water to make a workable dough.

2. Knead the dough and then cut into 8 pieces.

3. Place each piece between two pieces of wax paper and roll out to cracker thickness.

4. Prick the surface of each piece with the fork.

5. Bake on ungreased cookie sheets at 475° F for about 4 minutes. Turn the matzo over with the spatula and bake another 4 minutes until brown and crisp.

■ Matzo Balls

[Makes about 35 matzo balls]

Matzo ball soup is served during Passover, but it is a favorite the rest of the year as well.

Materials

3 tablespoons chicken fat
3 eggs
1 teaspoon salt
¼ teaspoon pepper

1 cup matzo meal
mixing bowl
spoon
simmering chicken broth

Procedure

1. Combine chicken fat and eggs in the bowl.

2. Add salt and pepper

3. Add enough matzo meal so that the mixture is slightly sticky.

4. Refrigerate for at least two hours.

5. With wet hands roll pieces of dough into balls about ¾ inch in diameter.

6. Drop into simmering chicken soup and cook for 15 minutes.

■ Rugela

[Makes 32 to 36 cookies]

Also spelled rugala and rugelach, these cookies are made all year long. However, they are very popular at Hanukah. Students who are allergic to nuts should not eat this recipe.

Materials

Dough:
  2⅓ cups flour
  ½ pound butter, softened
  1 cup sour cream
  mixing bowl
  mixing spoon
  plastic wrap
  extra flour
  rolling pin
  working surface with extra flour
  knife
  lightly greased cookie sheets

Filling:
  ⅓ cup sugar
  1 teaspoon sugar
  1 teaspoon cinnamon
  2 tablespoons finely chopped nuts
  small mixing bowl
  mixing spoon

Procedure

1. Combine 2 cups of flour, butter, and sour cream in the mixing bowl.
2. While stirring, add the last ⅓ cup of flour.
3. Shape into a ball and cover with plastic wrap.
4. Refrigerate overnight.
5. Remove from refrigerator and divide into 4 portions.
6. Lightly dust the working surface and place 1 of the 4 portions on surface.
7. Roll out into a circle about 12 inches in diameter.
8. Combine the ingredients for the filling in the small mixing bowl.
9. Spread 1 tablespoon of the filling on the dough circle.
10. Cut the dough like a pizza into sixteen triangles.
11. Start at the wide point of each triangle and roll to the point.
12. Repeat the process with the other pieces of dough.
13. Place on the lightly greased cookie sheets and bake at 350° F for about 15 minutes or until golden brown.

■ Hamantaschen
[Makes about 60 cookies]

Hamantaschen are eaten during Purim, a Jewish celebration. Esther, the Jewish wife of a king, saved the Jews from being destroyed by the evil advisor Haman. Purim occurs on the fourteenth or fifteenth day of the Jewish month Adar. Adar roughly corresponds to late February or March.

Materials

5 large eggs
1½ cups sugar
1 cup vegetable oil
½ cup orange juice
grated rind of 1 orange
grated rind of 1 lemon
1 tablespoon lemon juice
1 teaspoon vanilla
6½ cups flour
1½ teaspoons baking powder

½ teaspoon salt
3 cups fruit filling
2 large mixing bowls
whisk
mixing spoon
parchment paper
2 baking trays
rolling pin
working surface with extra flour
round cookie cutter, 3-inch diameter

Procedure

1. In a large mixing bowl beat the eggs with the whisk.

2. Slowly add the sugar, stirring constantly.

3. Add the oil, orange juice, lemon juice, vanilla, and grated rinds of orange and lemon.

4. In the other large mixing bowl combine the flour, baking powder, and salt.

5. Slowly stir the dry ingredients into the egg mixture.

6. Spread the dough on a parchment-lined baking tray. Cut the dough into quarters.

7. Refrigerate for at least 3 hours.

8. Remove one-fourth of the dough from the refrigerator.

9. Dust the working surface with flour and place dough on top.

10. Knead until smooth.

11. Roll out the dough with the rolling pin until the dough is ¼ inch thick.

12. Use the cookie cutter to make circles of dough.

13. Place the circles close together on a baking tray.

14. Use the scraps to make more circles.

15. Place a teaspoon of fruit filling into the center of each circle.

16. Fold over three sides of the dough around the filling.

17. Pinch dough to make triangles. Some of the fruit filling should be seen.

18. Bake at 350° F for 20 to 25 minutes or until the cookies are nicely browned.

19. Repeat the process with the rest of the refrigerated dough.

■ Easy Doughnuts
[Makes 24]

Students could make a "doughnut" chart (like a pie chart) of their favorite kinds of doughnuts.

Materials

3 cans 8-count refrigerated biscuits
knife
vegetable oil
frying pan and heating element, or
    electric skillet

plastic, resealable bags
powdered sugar

Procedure

1. Remove the biscuits from the cans and separate.
2. Use the knife to make a small hole in each biscuit.
3. Heat the oil in the frying pan to about 375° F.
4. Carefully drop the biscuits into the oil and fry.
5. Remove one at a time and let cool.
6. Pour powdered sugar into plastic bags.
7. Drop each doughnut one at a time into the powdered sugar and toss until coated.
8. Remove and enjoy.

■ Doughnuts from Scratch

[Makes about 30 doughnuts]

Doughnuts may not be nutritious, but they are good comfort food. Students could read Robert McCloskey's *Homer Price*. The book contains six stories, and one of them concerns a doughnut-making machine that gets out of control.

Materials

2 eggs
1 cup sugar
2 tablespoons melted butter
5 cups flour
3 teaspoons baking powder
¾ teaspoon nutmeg
¼ teaspoon salt
1 cup milk
cooking oil
powdered sugar (as optional topping)

mixture of 1½ teaspoons cinnamon and 2 tablespoons sugar (as optional topping)
large bowl
smaller bowl
mixing spoon
deep-fat fryer
large slotted spoon
paper towels

Procedure

1. Beat the eggs in the large bowl and add the melted butter and sugar.

2. Combine the flour, baking powder, salt, and nutmeg in the smaller bowl and then add to larger bowl.

3. Add the milk and combine.

4. Form 30 doughnuts.

5. Heat the deep-fat fryer to 375° F. Lower each doughnut gently into the oil with the large slotted spoon.

6. The doughnuts will rise to the surface of the oil when they are almost done. Cook a bit more.

7. Remove with the large slotted spoon and place on paper towels to drain.

8. Doughnuts may be sprinkled with powdered sugar or cinnamon-sugar mixture.

■ Welsh Griddle Cakes
[Makes about 24]

These are best eaten right away. That is usually not a problem!

Materials

1 cup sugar
4 cups flour
3 teaspoons baking powder
½ teaspoon salt
1 teaspoon nutmeg
3 sticks butter
1 cup currants or raisins
2 large eggs
2 tablespoons milk (if necessary)
1 cup confectioners' sugar

mixing bowl
mixing spoon
rolling pin
floured surface and extra flour
3-inch round cookie cutter
griddle
heating element
shortening for frying
cooling rack

Procedure

1. Combine the sugar, flour, baking powder, salt, nutmeg, and butter in the mixing bowl.

2. Stir in the currants or raisins.

3. Mix in the 2 large eggs.

4. A stiff dough should result. If necessary, add a bit of milk.

5. Roll the dough out on the flour surface until the dough is about ¼ inch thick.

6. Use the cookie cutter to make rounds. Gather the scraps and roll again until almost all the dough has been used.

7. Heat the griddle to a medium heat and grease the griddle with shortening. Cook the cakes on one side. They should rise a bit and become shiny.

8. Turn them over and cook the other side.

9. Place on the cooling rack and dust with the confectioners' sugar.

■ Crumpets

[Makes 10 to 12]

This traditional English bread is served with butter.

Materials

1 packet yeast
1 egg
2 cups lukewarm milk
¼ teaspoon salt
1 ounce butter
4 cups flour
2 small mixing bowls
1 large mixing bowl
whisk

2 mixing spoons
wax paper
working surface with extra flour
crumpet ring or clean tuna fish can with
  both ends removed
frying pan
heating element
extra butter for frying
spatula

Procedure

1. Mix yeast with ½ cup lukewarm milk in a small mixing bowl.

2. In the large mixing bowl combine the rest of the milk with the butter.

3. With the whisk beat the egg in a small mixing bowl and then add to milk-butter mixture.

4. Add the salt and 3 cups of flour. Mix well.

5. Add the yeast mixture and mix well again. Add more flour if necessary to form a dough.

6. Cover the dough with wax paper and allow the dough to rest in a warm location for 20 minutes.

7. Make 10 to 12 balls of dough and mold in the crumpet ring or tuna fish can "ring."

8. Place the crumpets on wax paper and allow to rise for 15 to 20 minutes.

9. Heat frying pan and add butter. Fry each crumpet for a couple of minutes on each side.

10. Serve warm. Split each crumpet and spread with butter.

■ Grandma's Buttermilk Pancakes
[Makes 12–14 pancakes]

This recipe has been in our family for generations. Neighborhood kids would come help us fix these pancakes.

Materials

2 cups flour	mixing bowl
1 teaspoon soda	mixing spoon
1 teaspoon salt	frying pan
1 tablespoon sugar	heating element
2 eggs	shortening for frying
about 1 cup buttermilk	spatula

Procedure

1. Combine the flour, soda, salt, and sugar in the mixing bowl.
2. Add the eggs and mix well.
3. Add about ½ cup buttermilk and combine. Add more buttermilk as necessary to make a thick batter.
4. Heat the frying pan and coat the bottom of the frying pan with shortening.
5. Pour in the pancakes. Flip them over when the edges are brown and the surface bubbles have broken.
6. Serve with butter and warm syrup.

■ Hoecakes
[Makes about 20]

Pioneers often made hoecakes as traveling food. They traveled well in food pouches (no honey or butter, though).

Materials

1 cup white cornmeal	frying pan and heating element, or
1¼ cups water	electric skillet
¾ teaspoon salt	spatula
mixing bowl	butter
mixing spoon	honey
vegetable oil	

Procedure

1. Combine the cornmeal and salt in the mixing bowl.
2. Add the water and mix.
3. Pour a small amount of oil into the frying pan.
4. When the oil is hot, pour in small amounts of the hoecake mixture.
5. Flip the hoecakes over with spatula when the bottom side is brown and crisp.
6. Serve with butter and honey.

■ Pita (Flat Bread)
[Makes 12]

Pita may have been the earliest type of bread to be made. Experts believe it started in the eastern Mediterranean region.

Materials

1 envelope yeast
1¼ cups lukewarm water
2 teaspoons honey
1 teaspoon salt
3 cups flour
½ stick butter

large bowl
mixing spoon
working surface and extra flour
cookie sheets
damp cloth

Procedure

1. In the large bowl combine the yeast, water, and honey. Let the mixture sit in a warm place for about 5 minutes or until it begins to bubble.
2. Stir in the salt and flour.
3. Knead the mixture on the working surface for 10 minutes.
4. Divide the dough into 12 pieces.
5. Pat each piece into a circle about 6 inches across and ¼ inch thick.
6. Butter the cookie sheets.
7. Lay the pitas on the buttered cookie sheets and cover with a damp cloth. Let rise in a warm place for about 45 minutes. They will puff up.
8. Remove the damp cloth and place in an oven.
9. Bake at 500° F for about 12 minutes. They should be lightly browned.

■ Chappatis (Indian Fried Bread)

[Makes 50 small chappatis]

Chappatis are sometimes served as an alternative to rice, and accompany many dishes. They can be frozen.

Materials

2 cups whole wheat flour
2 cups unbleached white flour
1 teaspoon salt
3 tablespoons oil or melted butter
butter for frying
about 2 cups water

mixing bowl
mixing spoon
working surface with extra flour
damp cloth
frying pan
heating element

Procedure

1. Combine the flours, salt, and oil.

2. Add enough water to make a stiff dough.

3. Knead for 5 to 10 minutes and then place the dough back in the bowl.

4. Cover the dough with a damp cloth and set it aside for an hour.

5. Shape the dough into balls the size of large marbles and then flatten each portion.

6. Fry each chappati over medium heat in a small amount of butter.

■ Crepes
[Makes 12 crepes]

A little crepe batter goes a long way.

Materials

1 cup flour
¼ teaspoon salt
1 cup milk
3 eggs
mixing bowl
whisk
mixing spoon

crepe pan or frying pan
heating element
oil
spatula
plate
sugar or jams (optional)

Procedure

1. With the whisk beat together the eggs, milk, and salt.
2. Add the flour, several teaspoons at a time. Beat until smooth and then add more flour. After all the flour has been added, the batter should be the consistency of light cream.
3. Heat the crepe pan or frying pan on high and add a small amount of oil. Turn down the heat to about medium.
4. Pour in about ¼ cup batter. Tilt the pan so that the batter spreads evenly across the pan.
5. When the edges brown, turn the crepe with the spatula.
6. Cook the other side and remove to a plate.
7. Cook the remaining crepes in the same way.
8. Sprinkle sugar or spread jam on each crepe and roll up.
9. Serve warm.

■ Navajo Fry Bread
[Makes 8 servings]

Shortening could be substituted for the lard.

Materials

3¼ cups flour
1 cup nonfat dry milk
1 tablespoon baking powder
½ teaspoon salt
10 ounces lard
1 cup ice water
1 teaspoon salt
mixing bowl
pastry blender

mixing spoon
towel
rolling pin
working surface with extra flour
knife
frying pan
heating element
spatula

Procedure

1. Combine the flour, nonfat dry milk, baking powder, and ½ teaspoon salt in the mixing bowl.
2. With the pastry blender cut in about 5 tablespoons lard. The mixture will resemble cornmeal.
3. Pour in the ice water and mix until the dough forms a large ball.
4. Cover with the towel and let stand at room temperature for about 2½ hours.
5. Divide the dough into 2 portions. Shape each piece into a ball and roll out on the floured surface until each is about ¼ inch thick.
6. Make 3 slits partway through the dough and let it rest again for about 10 minutes.
7. Heat the frying pan over medium-high heat and add some of the lard.
8. Place one of the dough circles in the hot oil and fry for about 4 to 5 minutes.
9. Flip the dough on the other side and fry again for about 4 to 5 minutes.
10. Remove the bread and drain on paper towels. Fry the other round.
11. Sprinkle both breads with salt and keep them warm. Cut into wedges when they are being served.

■ Sopapillas
[Makes 24]

Sopapillas are served as the end to a Mexican dinner in the American Southwest.

Materials

2 cups flour
1 teaspoon sugar
1 tablespoon baking powder
1 egg, beaten
1 teaspoon butter
1 cup milk
frying oil
mixing bowl
mixing spoon

working surface with extra flour
wax paper
rolling pin
frying pan
heating element
spatula
paper towels
honey or cinnamon-sugar mixture
    (optional)

Procedure

1. Combine the flour, sugar, and baking powder in the mixing bowl.
2. Add the egg, butter, and milk. Stir until the mixture looks like bread dough.
3. Knead well on floured surface for about 5 minutes.
4. Return dough to mixing bowl and cover with wax paper. Let stand for 2 hours.
5. Remove dough from bowl and roll out to ¼-inch thickness.
6. Cut dough into 4-inch squares.
7. Fry dough in hot oil for about a half minute per side. They cook quickly, and they puff up.
8. Drain on paper towels.
9. Serve hot with honey or cinnamon-sugar mixture.

■ Cinnamon Crisps
[Makes 48]

This treat is fairly healthy.

Materials

¼ cup sugar
2 teaspoons cinnamon
6 flour tortillas
3 tablespoons butter
mixing bowl
mixing spoon

microwave-safe bowl
microwave oven
basting brush
knife
cookie sheet

Procedure

1. Combine the sugar and cinnamon in the mixing bowl.
2. Melt the butter in the microwave-safe bowl in a microwave oven.
3. Brush both sides of each tortilla with butter. Sprinkle on the cinnamon and sugar.
4. Cut each tortilla into 8 pieces and place on cookie sheet.
5. Bake at 400° F for 5 to 7 minutes or until crisp.

■ Pemmican
[Makes about 3 cups, enough for about 12 students]

The original Native American fast food, the recipe called for buffalo fat instead of peanut butter. However, peanut butter is healthier and more appealing than animal fat. Make sure no student is allergic to nuts.

Materials

1 cup jerky
1 cup dried berries
1 cup roasted nuts
2 teaspoons honey
¼ cup peanut butter
other spices such as garlic powder or
    paprika to taste

food processor
spoon
small paper cups
disposable spoons

Procedure

1. Use the food processor to grind the jerky into a powder.
2. Add the dried berries and nuts.
3. Add the honey, peanut butter and other spices. Combine.
4. Distribute the mixture into the cups so that students can each have a taste.

26
Miscellaneous

■ Colorful and Fragrant Salt Map Dough
[Makes about 2 cups of one color]

This salt map dough contains color, so students will not need to paint it. The nice smell makes it fun to mold. Students use this dough to make salt maps, three-dimensional representations of geographic features. Students outline these features on a wood base and then sculpt the dough in the shape of the features. Salt maps take several days to dry.

Materials

1 small box of fruit-flavored gelatin
2 cups flour
about ¾ cup water

mixing bowl
mixing spoon

Procedure

1. Combine the gelatin and the flour in the mixing bowl.

2. Add a small amount of water to the mixture and combine.

3. Continue to add small amounts of water until the mixture resembles clay.

4. Mold and allow to dry.

■ Pine Needle Paintbrushes
[Makes 10]

Students can find out how commercial paintbrushes are made.

Materials

green pine needles
10 stocky twigs or small branches
10 pieces of string or yarn, each
    1 foot long

paint
paper

Procedure

1. Gather a number of pine needles and place around the end of the twig.

2. Tie in place with yarn or string.

3. Experiment with paint.

■ Newspaper Paintbrushes
[Makes 10]

Students can decide which paintbrushes work better, newspaper or pine needle (see above).

Materials

10 sturdy plastic straws
about 2 sheets newspaper
10 pieces of string or yarn, each
    1 foot long

paint
paper

Procedure

1. Tear the newspaper into about 12 small strips.

2. Place around the end of the straw.

3. Tie in place with yarn or string.

4. Experiment with paint.

■ Colored Sand
[Makes 1 cup]

This sand is far cheaper than colored sand purchased at craft stores.

Materials

1 cup sand or salt
3 teaspoons powdered tempera paint

airtight container

Procedure

1. Pour sand or salt and powdered tempera paint into the airtight container.

2. Cover and shake.

■ Decorative Plate

[Makes 1 plate]

Dollar stores are good sources for the glass plates.

Materials

1 clear glass plate
1 sheet white paper
scissors
markers or crayons
pencil

sponge brush
¼ cup white glue
¼ cup water
disposable cup

Procedure

1. Turn plate upside down and place white paper on the bottom.

2. Trace the bottom shape onto the white paper and cut out the shape.

3. Use the markers or crayons to create a decorative scene.

4. Pour the water and white glue into the disposable cup and mix.

5. Use the sponge brush to coat the bottom of the plate.

6. Place the picture onto the bottom of the plate so that when the plate is turned over the scene appears.

7. Let dry.

8. Coat with another layer or two of the white glue-water mixture.

9. Let dry again.

■ Quick Beanbags

[Makes 1]

Students can decide which filler is best.

Materials

1 small balloon
1 cup filler such as salt, flour, or sand

funnel

Procedure

1. Place the funnel in the balloon opening.

2. Pour in one of the fillings.

3. Remove the funnel and tie the balloon end.

4. Toss gently and have fun.

■ Saltwater Chalk
[Makes enough for 1 child]

Throw away the chalk after the activity. Different colors of chalks make a nice finished product.

Materials

disposable cup
2 teaspoons salt
¼ cup warm water

1 stick chalk
pale construction paper
mixing spoon

Procedure

1. Combine the salt and warm water in the disposable cup.

2. Dip the chalk into the warm salt water and let it remain there for about a minute.

3. Take it out and start to draw.

■ Crepe Paper Raffia
[Makes 1]

This takes a delicate hand.

Materials

1 crepe paper streamer
spool

Procedure

1. Twist the end of the crepe paper.

2. Carefully insert the end of crepe paper streamer through the hole of the spool.

3. Turn and pull length of crepe paper through the spool.

■ Rubber Stamp Ink and Pad
[Makes 1]

Watch out for the clothing dye. Obviously it can stain clothing. Rubber gloves may be a good idea here.

Materials

powdered clothing dye
¼ teaspoon rubbing alcohol*
5 tablespoons glycerin
disposable container such as a
    cottage cheese container

disposable spoon
plastic box with lid, such as a container
    for paper clips
piece of foam rubber the size of the
    bottom of the plastic box

*Rubbing alcohol should not be consumed. It is also flammable.

Procedure

1. In the disposable container combine the alcohol and enough dye to make a liquid the consistency of thin glue.

2. Add the glycerin.

3. Place the piece of foam in the bottom of the plastic box.

4. Pour the liquid onto the foam. Spread evenly with the disposable spoon.

5. Keep the lid on the plastic box tightly shut when the pad is not being used.

■ Sugar-Glitter Sun Catchers
[Makes about 8]

These can be made to match the seasons.

Materials

1 cup sugar	cookie sheet
4 teaspoons glitter	wax paper
2–3 teaspoons water	cookie cutters
mixing bowl	glue
mixing spoon	eight 12-inch pieces of thin ribbon

Procedure

1. Combine the sugar and glitter in the mixing bowl.
2. Add enough water to make the mixture stick together.
3. Line the cookie sheet with wax paper.
4. Place a cookie cutter on the wax paper.
5. Fill the cookie cutter with about 2 teaspoons of the material. Make sure to spread the material to a uniform thickness.
6. Gently remove the cookie cutter.
7. Repeat with other cookie cutters and the rest of the material.
8. Allow the shapes to dry overnight.
9. Glue the thin ribbon pieces onto the backs so that the sun catchers can be hung for display.

■ Sand Art
[Makes 1]

The more crayon, the better the final piece.

Materials

1 piece sandpaper	cookie sheet lined with aluminum foil
crayons	hot pad
oven	

Procedure

1. With the crayons create a scene on the piece of sandpaper. Press hard with the crayons.
2. Place the sandpaper on the aluminum foil-lined cookie sheet.
3. Bake in the oven at 350° F for about 20 minutes.
4. Remove from the oven and let cool.

■ Tissue Paper "Stained-Glass Windows"
[Makes 1]

These really brighten up a classroom. Liquid starch can be purchased at grocery stores.

Materials

colored tissue paper
liquid starch
wax paper

scissors
paintbrush
small container filled with water

Procedure

1. Cut small pieces of tissue paper and arrange on a piece of wax paper to form a picture.
2. Lift each piece one at a time and paint the underside with liquid starch.
3. Place the tissue paper back on the wax paper.
4. Clean brush when changing tissue paper color.
5. Let dry and hang from window.

■ Dyed Eggs Using Tissue Paper
[Makes 6]

The eggs should not be eaten because some of the tissue paper dye may not be safe to consume.

Materials

6 hard-boiled eggs
small pieces of brightly colored tissue
　paper

old paint brush
water in a small container
2 paper towels

Procedure

1. Paint the eggs with water.
2. Place small pieces of tissue paper all over the eggs.
3. Paint the tissue paper with more water so that the tissue paper is very wet.
4. Place the eggs on the paper towels and allow them to dry.
5. The tissue paper will fall off, and the eggs will be colored.

■ Indoor Mud Puddles

[Makes 1 large batch that can be used by several students]

Save the coffee grounds from the faculty room coffeepot for several days prior to this activity.

Materials

12 cups used and dry coffee grounds
1 container dry oatmeal

1 container salt
1 large, flat pan

Procedure

1. Pour the dry coffee grounds into the large, flat pan.

2. Allow students to play with the coffee grounds "mud puddles."

3. Allow students to add the oatmeal or salt to the coffee grounds and explore the differences.

■ Transfer Liquid

[Makes a bit more than ¼ cup, enough for quite a long time]

Use this mixture to transfer pictures from magazines or newspapers to paper to make projects. Comics are a great source of transfer material.

Materials

2 tablespoons soap powder (not detergent) or shavings from a bar of soap
¼ cup hot water
1 tablespoon turpentine*
disposable container, such as cottage cheese container

disposable mixing spoon
jar with screw top
picture
paper
old paintbrush
smooth rock or other object about the size of an egg

*Turpentine should not be consumed. It is also highly flammable.

Procedure

1. Combine the soap powder and hot water in the disposable container.

2. Add the turpentine.

3. Allow to cool and pour into jar. Screw on the top.

4. When ready to use, shake well. Paint a layer of liquid on the picture to be transferred. Wait about 10 seconds.

5. Place the paper over the picture and rub the area with the smooth rock. Wait a few seconds and then remove the paper. The picture should now be on the paper.

6. Sometimes pictures can be transferred more than once.

■ Mobile
[Makes 1]

Balancing the objects takes a bit of patience.

Materials

coat hanger
2 pencils or small dowels
string or yarn
8 objects to hang from mobile

scissors
hole punch
glue

Procedure

1. Punch a hole in the top of each of the eight objects.
2. Tie string through the holes. Leave a generous amount of string attached to each object.
3. Tie two objects to one pencil, one object at each end. Firmly attach by adding a bit of glue.
4. Tie two objects to the other pencil, one object at each end. Again firmly attach with a bit of glue.
5. Tie a piece of string to the middle of each pencil or dowel and secure with glue.
6. Tie the two pencils and the other four objects to the bottom of the coat hanger. Use various lengths of string so that the objects hang at various lengths.
7. Hold the coat hanger by the hook. Make sure the eight objects balance on the coat hanger. Move some if necessary.
8. Glue the strings to the coat hanger to keep everything in place.

Bibliography

Charner, Kathy, ed. *The Giant Encyclopedia of Art & Craft Activities for Children 3 to 6.* Beltsville, Md.: Gryphon House, 2000.

Charner, Kathy, ed. *The Giant Encyclopedia of Science Activities for Children 3 to 6.* Beltsville, Md.: Gryphon House, 1998.

Cobb, Vicki, and Kathy Darling. *You Gotta Try This! Absolutely Irresistible Science.* New York: Morrow Junior Books, 1999.

Hauser, Jill Frankel. *Kids' Crazy Concoctions: 50 Mysterious Mixtures for Art and Science Fun.* Charlotte, Vt.: Williamson Publishing, 1995.

Hauser, Jill Frankel. *Super Science Concoctions: 50 Mysterious Mixtures for Fabulous Fun.* Charlotte, Vt.: Williamson Publishing, 1997.

Hirschfeld, Robert, and Nancy White. *The Kids' Science Book: Creative Experiences for Hands-On Fun.* Charlotte, Vt.: Williamson Publishing, 1995.

Kohl, Mary Ann. *Mudworks: Creative Clay, Dough, and Modeling Experiences.* Bellingham, Wash.: Bright Ring, 1989.

Levenson, Elaine. *Teaching Children about Life and Earth Sciences.* New York: Tab Books, 1994.

Levenson, Elaine. *Teaching Children about Physical Science.* New York: Tab Books, 1994.

Marks, Diana. *Glues, Brews, and Goos: Recipes and Formulas for Almost Any Classroom Project.* Englewood, Col.: Teachers Ideas Press, 1996.

Milord, Susan. *Hands Around the World: 365 Ways to Build Cultural Awareness and Global Respect.* Charlotte, Vt.: Williamson Publishing, 1992.

Satler, Helen Roney. *Recipes for Art and Craft Materials.* New York: Lothrop, Lee & Shepard, 1973.

Thomas, John E. *The Ultimate Book of Kid Concoctions.* Strongsville, Ohio: The Kid Concoction Company, 1998.

About the Author

Diana Marks was born and raised in Colorado. Diana has been teaching for more than twenty-five years. She is currently employed by Council Rock School District, Bucks County, Pennsylvania, where she teaches gifted elementary students. She has taught every grade from first through eighth grade.

Diana resides in Washington Crossing, Pennsylvania, with her husband, Peter. They have two sons, Kevin and Colin. Diana loves to read, especially mysteries, and write. She also enjoys hiking and biking. She likes to travel, and she wishes her gardens were attractive enough to be photographed for a magazine.